THE NOVELS OF ARUN JOSHI

A CRITICAL STUDY

THE NOVELS OF ARUN JOSHI
A CRITICAL STUDY

Edited by

M.K. BHATNAGAR

ATLANTIC PUBLISHERS AND DISTRIBUTORS

Published by
ATLANTIC PUBLISHERS AND DISTRIBUTORS
B-2, Vishal Enclave, Opp. Rajouri Garden, New Delhi-27
Phones : 5413460, 5429987

Sales Office
4215/1, Ansari Road, Darya Ganj, New Delhi-110 002
Phones : 3273880, 3285873, 3280451
Fax : 91-11-3285873
e-mail : info@atlanticbooks.com
web : www.atlanticbooks.com

ISBN 81-269-0030-X

Typeset at
APD Computer Graphics, Delhi

Printed in India at
Mehra Offset Press, Delhi

PREFACE

Man evolves in interaction with other men and with the external reality objectified by his own self as well as by the selves of other beings around him. Literature, being but an artistic projection of the individual artist's perception, evolves likewise. The world of the novels of Arun Joshi is, in this sense, to be seen as a universe, transformed most subtly under the relentless pressure of the artistic legacy it inherited from the corpus of Joshi's predecessors. Consequently, Joshi's works call for not merely a focussed appraisal of their artistic contours but also a going back to the very climate which conditioned these contours. The present anthology seeks to undertake these twin-objectives equally vigorously, unearthing in the process facets of the 'strangeness' of Joshi's creations, hitherto barely touched or left unexplored. One cannot but incur immense intellectual debt in a number of quarters in the process. The editor acknowledges the invaluable help rendered by a number of scholars whom it is just not possible to personally thank. Without the immense support, encouragement and persistence — even in the face of seemingly unsurmountable odds — of Dr. K.R. Gupta, a fellow academic, the whole endeavour would not have seen the light of day. The whole project owes its existence to him.

M.K. BHATNAGAR

CONTENTS

1

"Beyond the Last Labyrinth : The Strange Case of Arun Joshi"

M.K. BHATNAGAR

Arun Joshi is incontrovertibly one of the foremost Indian writers exploring the nebulous labyrinths of self. It is as if a Bakha (*Untouchable*) or a Rahoul *(So Many Hungers*!) discard uncermoniously the external eye to let their own self unravel themselves. What results is an intriguing, though dazzling display of the multidimensional forces unleashed within, often mutually exclusive and seemingly illogical, irrational, inexplicable and charting out a personality that defies all known norms of 'civilized' behaviour. What can one say of a highly placed government official, Ratan Rathor by name, wiping clean the footwear of the devotees at the doorstep of a temple, or Billy Biswas, ditching a doting wife and a high academic position to walk seminaked in the wilderness? It is the capturing of this most elusive riddle of life in all its contrariness that distinguishes the fictional world of Arun Joshi. It is his insistent endeavour to capture the shades of life beyond the last labyrinth that makes the case of the novelist most strange. The matter as well as the manner of his novels is a world apart from his predecessors. Whereas Indian English fiction began as a saga of fables and romances, it came closer to contemporaneous concerns in the Gandhian era, with litterateurs setting their tales in a socially and politically recognizable milieu, it was only later that the focus shifted to the universe within from the world without. It was as if the protagonist, freed from the ubiquitous and pervasive shadow cast on his being by historical processes could be a wholesome self, for a change, and take stock of the ravages afflicted by the buffets of time which had tossed him helter-skelter although. While Lal Behari Day's *Govinda Samant* (1874) or S.C. Dutt's *The Young Zamindar* (1885) could only talk obliquely of their society or their own selves, S.K. Venkatraman's *Kandan the Patriot* (1932) or *Murugan the Tiller (*1927) or better still Raja Rao's *Kanthapura* (1938) or Mulk Raj Anand's Coolie (1936) or Manohar Malgonkar's *A Bend in the Ganges* (1964) dared to talk explicitly about the scars left on the individual as well as on the society he was a part of under the colonial regime. However, it was only a Maya (in Anita Desai's *Cry, the Peacock*, 1963) or Sita in *Where Shall We Go This Summer*?, 1975) and, in continuation thereof, a Ratan in Arun Joshi's *The Apprentice* (1974) or a Sindi Oberoi in his *The Foreigner* (1968) who could impulsively and inevitably detach themselves from these 'extraneous' concerns, corrosive of the self-sufficiency of the individual and look at the mystery of life detachedly, without being overawed by its dreadful and unnerving aura.

What is the vista beyond the last labyrinth in Arun Joshi's fictional world all about? What lies at the core of this strange universe created in his novels? What is so unusual, unexpected, abnormal or even absurd herein? Going back to the well-known formation in existentialism, "absurd is that which is devoid of purpose ... Cut off from his religious, metaphyscial and transcendental roots, man is lost; all his actions become senseless, absurd, useless."[1] One may speculate and isolate a number of factors which might lead to such a scenario : the dominance of sheer, ahuman technology over human aspirations and perceptions, howsoever 'petty', trivial and personal; the collapse of the world of fixities and the endless agony of waiting for the precipitation of a new set of values, born out of new experiences and contexts or the alarmingly escalating ennui, consequent upon the gratification of all hungers, howsoever voracious, leading to the complacency — annihilating and spiritually — disquieting poser — whither now. The resultant mental anguish at the meaninglessness of the human condition is at the core of Arun Joshi's ouevre.

The Apprentice, Which the novelist claimed was his favourite,[2] has not received the kind of critical attention it deserves. This gap in scholarship is sought to be bridged by A. Rajendra Prasad and Pier Paolo Piciucco, who in their articles, devoted to the content and the form of the novel respectively, bring to light aspects of the novel hitherto left unexplored. A Rajendra Prasad's "After the Fall" : A critque on Arun Joshi's *The Apprentice* is a highly sensitive study of Ratan Rathor, the protagonist as he confronts the spiritual chaos within his being. "Fictional Technique and Rhetorical Devices in Arun Joshi's *The Apprentice* is a painstaking analysis of the manner wherein the novelist seeks to highlight as well as accentuate the crises the protagonist undergoes during the intermittent course of his evolution. Such stylistic studies are conspicuous by their absence in the Indian English critical scene and, therefore, the effort by the critic in this infrequently explored direction is most praiseworthy. *The Foreigner* is another novel which has been looked at only thematically, ignoring the rich critical insight formalistic forays into the novel can yield. The article on the novel, included in the present anthology is also content-based but the aspect of the them taken up here is rather fresh. Shivani Vatsa and Rashmi Gaur in "The Concept of Humane Technology in Arun Joshi's : *The Foreigner*" highlight the ahuman face of modern science and technology which has dislocated man from his environment and sowed seeds of anomic, alienation and nausea. Nothingness has enveloped, the ensuing gap between 'being for itself' and 'being in itself'.

The Strange Case of Billy Biswas, perhaps Arun Joshi's most well-known novel, reveals a seemingly schizophrenic protagonist within whom reside relatively compatibly a modern intellectual as well as a primitive — an incarnation of the Jungian unconscious, one can perhaps hazard. This equipoise is threatened and rendered untenable by the shrill demands made on the protagonist's 'civilized self' by his 'natural' self and despite his sincere efforts to keep sailing in the two streams, flowing in reverse directions, his very existence is smothered by the intervention of extraneous forces. Urmil's study of the novel, entitled "Quest for Self in Arun Joshi's *The Strange Case of Billy Biswas*" seeks to link up these two seemingly severed selves by focusing on the protagonist's discomfiture with modern civilization and his being drawn to the natural, the spontaneous and the raw at the very outset itself. The denonuement, then, becomes but a foregone conclusion wherein the jungle would ultimately claim him and all efforts to thwart that would succeed only in complicating the picture. It is this rootedness to the soil which nurtures and nourishes the soul. Technology, by its very abstraction and voracious instinct to master and tame Nature, pitts man not merely against his immediate environment but also against his inner self and this 'unequal' confrontation has but a predictable fate : the inexorable annihilation of the individual self from within in most cases. That is precisely the thrust of Shivani Vatsa and Rashmi Gaur's article entitled "A study of the Corrupting Influence of Technology : *The Strange Case of Billy Biswas*".

The Last Labyrinth is in many ways a continuation and an extension of the quest-motif that characterizes all of Joshi's novels, wherein a seemingly 'abnormal' protagonist is sensitised one way or the other towards the alternative reality, relegated to the background in the pursuit of the worldly, though ephemeral reality. The graph hereafter varies, depending upon the nature and circumstances of the protagonists concerned, but the highest common factor, in each case, involves an unrelenting endeavour to capture the most elusive nuance, to penetrate the most inaccessible and impregnable layer of the mystery of life. M. Mani Meitei in "Indian Ethos in Arun Joshi's *The Last Labyrinth*" isolates and highlights the quintessentially Indian beliefs, myths, cultural, social and spiritual imprints and ways of thinking. The study also dilates upon the manner wherein all these ingredients combine and coalesce to create artistically the very ethos of the novel. In another study the discontent searing the very soul of Som, the protagonist in the novel has been subjected to a sustained scrutiny to diagnose its origin, nature and consequences. M. Rajeshwar and B. Brahmananda Chary in "Orchestra of Discontent : Som's Quest in *The Last Labyrinth*" traces the inner craving of the individual self eating into the very heart of seeming felicity. Som is but a metaphor defining in his own inimitable manner the slow but steady anagnorisis which each 'gifted' being is destined to face, sooner rather than later, on his pulse. This anagnorisis concerns the choice to be made between the two mutually exclusive facets of reality — one of which man is the creator and the other where man himself is but a creature. Shubha Tiwari's Race Consciousness in Arun Joshi's *The Last Labyrinth*" is another sustained study of facets of consciousness in the novel, hitherto left unexplored. S.S. Rangachari in "Islolation" in Arun Joshi's *The Foreigner* and *The Last Labyrinth*" is a comparative study of the two novels, highlightin the manner wherein the sense of alienation, rootlessness and 'otherness' contribute meaningfully to the making of the two protagonists. Isolation precipitates the inchoate rumblings of perception in these potentially sensitive beings and it is isolation, again, which leads them to a higher and fuller awareness of life in its pristine mystery. K.M. Pandey examines Joshi's last novel in "Symbol as Strucutre : Arun Joshi's *The City and the River*" and discovers therein continuation of the same thematic concerns in a new context and format.

In the last section of the anthology, focus is an a critically inclusive perspective whereby the entire corpus of the novelist is examined. S.P. Swain and S. Samartary juxtapose Ratan, Som, Sindi Oberoi and Billy Biswas among others to iterate the common strains in their questing selves, tormented by alienation. The study concerned is "The Problem of Alienation and the Quest for Identity in Arun Joshi's Novels." Continuing the over-all critical analysis Mallikarjun Patil in "Arun Joshi's Fictional Forte" takes up for detailed consideration the distinguishing attributes of the novelist's concerns as well as the formalistic devices deployed by him.

Arun Joshi's strange case, then involves an increasingly ahuman world wherein the individual protagonist discovers to his chagrin, nothingness enveloping each aspect of the external reality. Thoroughly frustrated they seek to catch at a straw and construct some semblance of meaning, some connectedness, rootedness, howsoever, tenuous which could facilitate the wiping of the 'nauseating' smog which obstructs their perspective. Striving for newer values and stances in a chamcleon-like changing and obfuscating reality, man pulls at the absurdity of all his actions in conformity with the reality without, for this meaninglessness, purposelessness and nothingness emanates from the very heart of his being — "like a worm." The present anthology of critical studies has endeavoured to graph the distinctive strategies taken recourse to by Joshi's protagonists to step out of the soul –sucking cycle of Circe. These incisive forays into the strange world of Joshi often contain insights into diverse facets of the individual's dilemma hitherto but scratched or left absolutely unexplored. Only the connoisseurs can say how far the endeavour has succeeded.

NOTES AND REFERENCES

1. Eugene Ionesco, "Dans Les armes de la Ville," *Cahiers de la Compagnie Madeleine Renaud*, Jean-Louis Barrault, Paris, No. 20, October 1957.
2. Quoted in Puraby Banerjee, "A Winner's Secrets," *The Sunday Statesman*, 27 February 1983.
3. Jean-Paul Sartre, *Being and Nothingness*, trans. Hazel E. Barnes (New York : Washington Square Press, Pocket Books, 1966), p. 56.

2

"After the Fall" : A Critique on Arun Joshi's *The Apprentice*

A. RAJENDRA PRASAD

The portrayal of Ratan Rathor, the protagonist of Arun Joshi's *The Apprentice* (1974), is an artistic transcript of the self-made man's steep fall in morals in proportion to his meteoric rise in material status. He is simultaneously a product and a victim of the decadent social values that gave a fillip to his ambition and rendered him deaf to the voice of his own conscience. Saddled by the dichotomy in his 'double inheritance', and regretful of having misguidedly pursued the false philosophy of 'becoming one with the society around on its own terms', he becomes a near nervous wreck under the strain of salvaging a modicum of self-respect on which he is to rebuild the edifice of the remaining years of his life.

Ratan's regret is that his whole life had been a total waste, a great mistake without purpose, without results. This is best reflected in his sad comment to the student : "There are many sorrows in the world, but there is nothing in the three worlds to match the sorrow of a wasted life" (140). Ratan is thus a protagonist typical of Arun Joshi in so far as his most sincere effort, however belated, was to be in right relation with his own inner sense of *dharma*.

The novel traces four distinct phases in Ratan's life : the phase of youth and idealism, phase of adulthood and coming up in life the hard way, the phase of disillusionment and guilt, and finally the phase of repentance and atonement. His father's life of service and his courageous martyrdom in the cause of Indian independence left a deep imprint on Ratan's impressionable mind and he genuinely tried to emulate his father's example. His toying with the idea of joining Subash Chandra Bose's army, his sincere wish to "lay the foundation of a glorious future" (21), his dream of the great tasks awaiting him, his feeling suffused with pride and happiness at the prospect of sacrificing his all without the promise of a reward, as if some "vital essence" (22), within him manages to break out and lose itself in something that was bigger and beyond him, establish how deep rooted is his identification with his father and how important it for him to be respected like him.

Added to this is the natural psychological need of the child to win maternal admiration for uncommonly heroic achievements. But in the last minute, the memory of his father's death, instead of strengthening his decision to join the army, demoralises him and he fails to enlist his name as a soldier. He weeps in humiliation, ashamed of his own cowardice. This reminiscence, accompanied by his agonised comment, "And there are memories whose sting neither time nor words can heal. They burrow in the body of your soul, like maggots, wriggling, mocking, green forever" (22), through shows the tragedy of the unbridgeable gap between the worlds of reality and of dreams.

Early in his struggle for survival, Ratan realises that to be the son of a martyr is of no earthly use in getting a job and the harsh reality of his father's leaving being him 'a cynical widow and her illness' and 'plenty of patriotic fervour and precious little funds' shatters his ego. Bullied and mocked, he visits office after office to be "examined, interviewed, interrogated and rejected" (20). He almost dies of starvation but is rescued by his room mates. A fortuitous introduction by one of them fetches him a temporary job in the department of war-purchases and that small foot-holds is cleverly used by Ratan to reach the high point of his career till he has all the paraphernalia of material success. Ratan's achieving this prosperity through "perfidy, chicanery, cowardice and corruption" (Abraham 212), is quite in tune with the decadent society around him "a society without norms, without direction, without even, perhaps, a purpose" (Joshi 74). Ratan's carefully cultivated ingratiating manner and perfect yes-manship soon make him a valued employee and the upward rise in his career is accepted by him as recognition of his own merit : "I was a different cut :

educated, intelligent, cultured, and it was my right that I should rise in life, to levels higher than the others aspired for" (32). He blots out from his mind his poverty-stricken past and feels no compunction in shedding the friends and associates of that time, including those who saved his life.

Ratan's smug self-satisfaction receives a jolt when the contractor's son tries to buy his support with a bribe of ten thousand rupees. Ratan is shocked that the same world which once bullied one should servilely seek to grease his palms to get things done to suit to its interests.

The superintendent's offer of 'officership' to Ratan as a reward for marrying his niece marks a turning point in his life. The initial qualms he feels about degrading marriage to the level of a 'deal', and his subsequent consent to it, show that with his new understanding of deals he has indeed become a fit officer in a system that has come venerate 'deals' as a new gospel :

> If men forgot how to make deals the world, would come to a shop. It would lose it's propelling power. Men would not know what it do with themselves. ... It is not the atom or the sun or God or Sex that lies at the heart of the Universe : it is deals. DEALS. It is a bit like my mother's prophecy, about money. It is not whether you like making deals or you like money. They are simply there, like air (51).

During the war he becomes conspicuously patriotic. He emerges as the most willing and enthusiastic donor of blood in his locality and when no newspaper publishes his pedantic article on fall of moral standards in post-independence India, he gets copies of it cyclostyled and gets them distributed all over the town. The height of hypocrisy is to be found in lashing at corruption in India while all the time he was trying to sort-out in his mind his reasons for accepting a huge bribe.

Bottled up tensions are bound to explode sooner or later, and that is what happens in Ratan's tussle with his higher self. As a forewarning of the psychic cataclysm about to take place in his life, Ratan begins to experience bouts of restlessness, apathy and discontent that leave him a frustrated man in the family and a lethargic indifferent employee in the office.

By the time Ratan wakes up to the fact that in the process of adjustment unacceptable to his higher self, something fine in his own soul is destroyed, things have already gone from bad to worse, and he finds himself cornered into a veritable moral aridity with no company other than of his own fury.

To his dismay, Ratan has to realise that his role, in connivance with the fraudulent arms dealer, Himmat Singh, in clearing the defective war weapons, has caused the death of the Brigadier. He has the visions of the Brigadier standing "sleepless and exhausted, in a show-bound trench, hemmed in by machine guns... " (56).

But Ratan proves too smooth a customer to be unnerved by the interrogations of the army official or the Superintendent of Police. By a phone call to Himmat Singh, he succeeds in getting orders for his release. The Superintendent of Police makes a mocking reference to his influential friends but tells him point blank that the Brigadier is facing court-martial on charges of desertion and his only chance of acquittal was in Ratan's confession.

As if moved by the words of the Superintendent of Police, Ratan prepares a letter of carefully-worded confession with enough loopholes for him to wriggle his way out, once the Brigadier's name is cleared. Needless to say, he never sends the confession to the Superintendent of Police. And after two weeks, he comes to know that the Brigadier had shot himself dead. When he goes to console the bereaved widow of the Brigadier, she hands him back the 'charm' he gave his friend on the eve of departure for battlefield. Hearing that it was the Brigadier's express wish that it should be returned to him, Ratan is strangely moved. After visiting the mutilated head of the Brigadier at mortuary, in a fit of fury, he goes to the house of Himmat Singh to kill him. For all his melodramatic threatening stance and solemn lecturing, Ratan is deflated when informed by Himmat Singh that the minister and the secretary were the instigators of the plot to make a fast buck out of the arms deal.

Later, Himmat Singh tells him of his childhood days, of poverty and privation, of one sister running away from home, the other dying of pneumonia and his own taking up a variety of odd jobs to make both ends meet. Regarding his present occupation of a 'racketeer', he expresses total satisfaction as it gives him an outlet for his hatred against society. Accusing Ratan of 'botching up his inheritance', Himmat expresses regret for nearly driving his mother crazy by his disregard of her warning about "getting entrenched in God's darkness" (145). Ratan recollects talking to him about God late into the night. He particularly recalls Himmat Singh's telling him that, may be, the only cure for God's darkness is God himself. Himmat Singh remarks,

> My soul was killed, you put yours to pawn. But souls that were pawned could perhaps be retrieved... May be souls are like muscles, Ratan Rathor. May be to develop them one has first to put them to use... Try to put yourself to use... It might be too late. You have been too long the slave... But give it a try (146-47),

have a profound impact on Ratan and are largely responsible for the change in his outlook on life. Acutely feeling the need for God's grace in restoring peace to his trouble-torn life, Ratan tries to do penance for his misdeeds by going to the temple every morning on his way to the office and wiping the shoes left near the threshold by the devotees who have gone into pray. Even the memory of shoes, according to Ratan, acts as a check on his lapsing into his old ways :

> And during the day whenever I find myself getting to be clever, lazy, vain, indifferent, I put up my hands to my face and there is the smell of a hundred feet that must at the moment be toiling somewhere and I am put in my place (149).

Ratan's unsparing criticism of his own failings is part of the cleansing process, the real goal of all confessions. Ostensibly, Ratan's is a story of success. Since his name is cleared, by interferences from highest levels, there is no stigma attached to his name as far as the world is concerned. All the accusations of moral lapse stem from his own conscience while for all practical purposes, he continues to be treated by the world as an honoured citizen. There is no danger of his being suspended from his job. The death of the Brigadier removed any fear there might have been of Ratan's being found guilty, and interestingly, this knowledge triggers off Ratan's confession instead of encouraging him to keep the secret locked for ever in the recesses of his own heart.

A prosecutor normally accuses the defendant in the interests of the public but here the curious emergence of Ratan as the 'accused', the judge and the prosecutor suggests a reality of such complex dimensions, that conventional terms of expression cannot convey it. Arun Joshi's use of the phrase 'green forever' may be cited as an example. This phrase, normally used to indicate something pleasant, something whose eternity is wished for, is used by Arun Joshi to bring out the inevitable disintegration of the psyche when thrown a prey to the maggots of accumulated frustrations.

'Wiping of shoes' has symbolic overtones of the Christian concept of Christ's washing the feet of his disciples on Mandy Thursday. Only humility could help Ratan to get rid of all the delusions that made his life 'an endless torrent of fear'.

Ratan's acute awareness of his inner void and his reference to his various foolish acts as futile bids to fill it — "one never knows what emptiness lies within one and which, when the time comes, one would fill up with muck" (89) — suggest the possibility of even the shoe-shining is being one more act of 'filling the void with muck'.

The failure of the act of penance to have any curative effect whatsoever on his fractured self is owned by Ratan himself : "And I was used up. That in a nutshell was the matter with me, still is, for that matter, in spite of all the rigmarole that I go through every morning" (68).

The enigmatic reference to his own solemn act of penance as a rigmarole by no other than the repentant himself points to a lack of seriousness. At the same time, instead of throwing additional light, it only complicates the riddle of Ratan's penitance in so far as his continuing with it is concerned. It is a self-prescribed act, as he was not answerable to anyone, and could easily have discontinued it, particularly when, according to his own admission, it did not produce any salutary chance. It can mean only one thing — he still has hopes of its curing him and is prepared to wait. Even when everything is lost 'the future still remains,' and it is a measure of Ratan's courage that instead of running away from the mess he made of his life, he takes the first step in setting things right.

The poojari's trying to buy his cooperation in settling the charges against his son, the contractor caused such a revulsion in Ratan that he made it a point never to enter a temple again : "The closest I come is the threshold where they leave the shoes" (124). As for his choosing that particular temple, Ratan's explanation was simple.

It had come to have a sentimental value for him, as it was to that temple he was led by the hobbling Himmat Singh and shown the slum area behind it — "so vast a slum, in fact, that its edges are not known to the ordinary citizen" (142). Himmat Singh started his life here as a shoes-shine boy and may be that prompted Ratan to choose shining of shoes as his means of expiation. The enigma here is that just as Himmat Singh's first job, 'his apprenticeship in making a living,' is shining of shoes, Ratan's first job in his apprenticeship to right living is also the same. Only he takes it up not to become like Himmat Singh but to avoid ending up like him.

Ratan's daily visits to the hospital to enquire about the Brigadier's welfare, as his desire to be seen waiting with the crowd outside newspaper office to hear about the war news he can easily get from the media even by staying at home, point to an element of duplicity reminiscent of Clemence, the hero of Camus' famous novel, *The Fall.*

Like Camus, Joshi also seems to be trying to make his hero simultaneously a 'portrait, mask and mirror' of the modern man, baffled as much by the loss of parameters to judge right from wrong, as by the absence of moral values. Though Ratan is not shown as eagerly pouncing on all tourists to 'confess' so that he can have the perverse pleasure of proving that all are guilty, he more than once admits to a pathetic need for an audience to whom he can unburden himself. His saying that it is nice to have the student to talk to, highlights another feature of the modern man-lack of human-level communication. Ratan also does not practise the psychological ruse of Clemence to judge others before they can judge him. If Ratan's stifling of conscience is inexcusable, his genuine repentance, and his refusal to allow his guilt to paralyse his will to run a new leaf is highly commendable. In direct contract to Clemence's relieved cry, "A second time, eh, what a risky suggestion... It's too late now. It'll always be too late. Fortunately" (Camus 108-09), Ratan welcomes a second chance with the sincere conviction : "One must try and not lose heart, not yield, at any cost to despair" (Joshi 149).

WORKS CITED

Abraham, Joy, "Vision and Technique in *The Apprentice*". *The Fictional World of Arun Joshi*. Edited by R.K. Dhawan, New Delhi : Classical, 1986.

Camus, Albert, *The Fall*, Tr. J.O'Brien, London : Hamish Hamilton, 1957.

Joshi, Arun, *The Apprentice*, New Delhi : Orient Paperbacks, 1974.

3

Fictional Technique and Rhetorical Devices in Arun Joshi's *The Apprentice*

PIER PAOLO PICIUCCO

Indian fiction in English has suffered for a long time the unjust destiny of the unimportant one among the post-colonial literatures. Only in recent times has it found its real place in the consideration of the critics at an international level : as a consequence, there has been a considerable, sometimes immodest, interest and re-evaluation of themes and authors so far unnoticed. There are few doubts, however, that among the authors forgotten in the shadows, Arun Joshi is a major name. Though winner of the Sahitya Academi Award in 1983, he never found the right fulcrum to climb the scale of success. One can possibly ascribe this fact to two basic reasons : the first is that at the time Arun Joshi wrote, Penguin India had still not made its grand and messianic entry on the scene and he was, therefore, printed by minor publishers. The second is that he himself was an introvert and reserved person : in his own words, he didn't "consider [himself] connected with the world of writers"[1]. The result is that, although his value is generally acknowledged by the restricted circle of scholars, his name paradoxically remains unknown to a wider audience as his novels are sadly out of print or, worse still, victims of a careless distribution which leaves large parts of India out of its range. The declared aim of this paper is to try to cast light on a very skilled and compulsive writer.

The Apprentice (1974) somehow emblematises its author's limited fame as it is quite neglected among the works of Joshi himself. Published between *The Strange Case of Billy Biswas* (1971), Arun Joshi's most famous novel, and *The Last Labyrinth* (1981), which won him the Sahitya Akademi Award, it is a real masterpiece and a most compelling work of art. It relates the story of the feverish pursuit of a career by Ratan Rathor, a senior officer at the Ministry of Defence, during the Indo-Chinese conflict. Starting from the arrival and the hard beginning in Delhi up to the attainment of a leading role, the reader follows the protagonist's climbing of the social scale achieved through the recurrent use of manoeuvres. By the same token, the portrait of the various strata of the society which he happens to deal with, becomes gradually gloomier and gloomier, depicted as they are with quite a pessimistic tone. That, though, is not without a reason. Ratan Rathor, in fact, remains entangled in a sordid business with catastrophic consequences. He accepts a huge bribe to clear a defective supply of' war material from Himmat Singh, a character of astonishing impact who ultimately reveals himself as a sort of Ratan's *alter-ego*. Even though all the documents which materially prove Ratan's active involvement in the deal are destroyed, the protagonist has to face problems with justice. His stubborn obstination to deny every accusation on his part leads him out of jail; yet, he remains defenseless in the face of his conscience. The substandard lot of weapons he has cleared, in fact, once on the front, is the cause of a massive defeat of the Indian army which, in terms of human lives, counts many hundreds of losses. Among them there is the Brigadier, Ratan's old best friend, who deserts to avoid death; while waiting for his trial he commits suicide, an act that Ratan's confession that a defective lot of war materials had been sent to the front would have surely avoided, proving as it would his friend's innocence. The protagonist undergoes a deep crisis which he finally resolves to overcome by rescuing his soul; every day he now goes to the temple to polish the shoes of the devotees and becomes an apprentice of God, hence the title.

The fictional technique adopted by Arun Joshi is surely one of the primary motivations of uniqueness in *The Apprentice*. Albeit some connotations clearly make direct or indirect reference to various other sources, *The Apprentice* is a very original novel in its structure, so that the critic V.V.N. Rajendra Prasad classifies it as "a fictional experiment."[2] In a very ingenious way, Ratan narrates the facts of his own life to a listener, whose name we ignore; what is relevant is that of the imaginary dialogue between the two of them, the novel only records the voice of the protagonist. It is as though one were listening to a person talking to the phone; one would not hear the interlocutor's voice, but would presumably understand his/her remarks, questions and general comments from the reactions of the person nearby. Consequently, one finds it difficult to agree with the general assumption that this novel is rendered in the form of a "monologue"[3] but, rather, in a most peculiar way of fictionalising a dialogue. Nor, as Joy Abraham states, does the narrator address himself to "an imaginary companion"[4] but to a real character. One may be deceived by the fact that this figure tends to metaphorically represent the implied reader; there are few doubts, anyway, that the listener, who is a National Cadet and a student, has clear-cut features. As the story unfolds, we come to know him very well : he is young, well-mannered, sensible, generous, an idealist, proud to be a National Cadet. He always pays great attention to every detail he is told, so that if Ratan gets confused while digressing and forgets what he was relating, he helps him to find the thread of his thoughts. His questions are wise and sharp so that Ratan calls him "young inquisitor";[5] even if he has to go to study for his examinations, he patiently waits for Ratan to conclude his episode. Since he is inexperienced in the ways of the world — "untouched"[6] as the narrator says — and always reveals goodness of heart, Ratan calls him confessor.[7] In short, no one better than he could interpret the role of the interlocutor : he is "a patient listener."[8] The fact that he does not possess a name, does not mean that he is symbolical. The gloomy, Kafkaesk atmosphere of the novel tends to ignore the identity of every character so that the reader knows them through their social role or kind of relationship to Ratan. The characters of *The Apprentice* are, in fact, the Superintendent, the Secretary, my wife, my daughter, the two Mirzapur brothers, a government engineer, the M.P., the S.P. Not even his best friend has a name : we come to know him as the Brigadier. The only exception to this rule is Himmath Singh, whom, anyway, Arun Joshi hastens to define "a man without a name."[9]

Another seminal topic one has to scrutinize when dealing with the fictional technique and rhetorical devices in *The Apprentice* is the nature of the conversation. If the author has then characterised the good-hearted and innocent student as an ideal listener, on the other hand, he also succeeds into portraying Ratan Rathor as a remarkable orator. The extremely effective dynamics of the novel basically lies on the fact that Ratan-narrator and Ratan-character are two different personae. A dramatic series of painful events have marked a drastic turning point in his life. As a result, the absorbing narration in the first person is sometimes connoted by a detachment one is rather accustomed to find in a third person's. Anyway, the control of the distance from the object of the narration is not so steady as Ratan would like. He is often carried away by sentimentalisms, a process he deeply regrets and for which he also begs his pardon. As an orator, therefore, Ratan is at his best. One must credit the critic C.N. Srinath with a perceptive insight as he rightly points out :

> The contrast between the earlier Ratan, the apprentice who has hitched his wagon to the star of success, and Ratan the apprentice who has passed through the dark night of soul, is brought out in anger, remorse and intense suffering that one can feel in the tone of the narration.[9]

Ratan not only talks, but becomes active part of his speeches : he laughs, broods, sings, shouts, goes into tantrums and it is not impossible to imagine him goggling his eyes at various points in the narration. Joshi has a large recourse to artifices to reproduce these rhetorical features. An extensive exploiting of repetitions, such as in "Ah, my friend, we know and we know and we know but what do we do with what we know"[10], is made throughout the novel. Another widely used stratagem is to have recourse to the capitalisation of words so as to magnetize the interlocutor's attention and to graphically render a peak of tension during the narration. In the following example we find it accompanied by the use of repetitions :

> Deals, deals, deals, my friend, that is what the world runs on, what is all about. If men forgot how to make deals the world would come to a stop. It would lose its propelling power. Men would not know what to do with themselves. They would lose interest. It is not the atom or the sun or God or sex that lies at the heart of the universe : it is DEALS. DEALS.[11]

The brooding nature of his recollections directly fishes from painful memories over which Ratan still has no control. It is, therefore, quite recurrent to read passages made out of extremely short sentences — that rarely put five words together —, symbolising the mood and the psychological weakness of the orator who, we may imagine, almost talks undertone in such occurrences. This is an example :

> The wide world and me. Me and the wide world. But how can one separate the two. The wide world took me in its wake, overwhelmed me, smothered me. As simple as that. I am no giant. A pigmy, if anything. One of those dwarfs that follow the processions. At best a bystander.

This stratagem appears still more evident if we compare the quotation above to a moment of enthusiasm, when the memory of happy moments completely floods the narration, so that we may imagine Ratan smiling, radiant.

> There were other things that we did, things that young men do, things without meaning, except the meaning they acquire when youth is spent. What meaning is there in cycling ten miles, towards the setting sun, your hand on another man's shoulder or swimming across a river before dawn or going to village fairs to look at the girls, or sitting in a mangrove all day preparing for examinations but, in fact, talking only sex, week after week. Or laughing at nothing until tears roll down your cheeks.[12]

There are two more rhetorical devices which fully reveal the writer's intention to reach climaxes quite abruptly. The first is the orator's adoption of questions which make the listener/reader take direct part in the narration. This method is concomitant with descriptions of tragic events; lest the interlocutor miss the extreme seriousness of the predicament, Ratan rhetorically overcharges his interpellation with an *ever*, so as to emphasise that the occurrence he is relating has a uniqueness which is out of the question :

> Have you ever lived with someone tubercolar?[13]
> Have you ever had the feeling that you were choking?[14]
> Have you ever been to the Military Hospital?[15]
> Have you, my friend, have you ever seen men on the brink of madness?[16]

The other device Joshi makes use of aims at reaching a similar effect. All of a sudden he starkly characterises his personae by making them answer in a most odd and unexpected way to questions that are addressed to them or, alternatively, by starting talking about a plain subject in a very strange manner. Since the author never casts doubts of madness over them, but rather hints that beyond the surfacing strangeness of their sentences lies the crux of the matter, the reader's attention abruptly reaches a peak in order to solve the dilemma. This appears as a very effective technique in that it transfers the element of surprise from the orator to the reader out of the blue. In the following case Ratan is chatting with the Brigadier.

> As solicitous as you please, I had asked him if something was the matter. He had not answered me. Instead, he had started to talk of something very different.

After focussing upon the characteristics of both the narrator and the interlocutor, it would he worth analysing the nature of their relationship. Their first meeting at the beginning of the novel is accidental, but one may soon notice how reciprocally well-disposed the two of them instinctively are. More than that, their relationship is marked by insincerity and affection. Starting from these premises and considering the generational gap which divides the two actors on the stage, one may set their interaction on the same line of that of a father and a son. Ratan expressly makes a vague reference to this point at the beginning of the novel when he states "You are after all a student, almost like my son, had I had one."[17] The confessional story that constitutes the structure of the novel is not an end in itself but, apart from the expiating role that it acquires by simply mentioning it, it is meant as a lesson for his listener. Regarding this point, the critic T. Guruprasad connects the two roles of the narration into a single continuum :

> It is worthy of critical attention that this novel is also in the confessional mode. As a matter of fact, the narrator in this novel is an insistent confessionalist, confession is a factor in his redemption, for Ratan has got hold of a young man, an apprentice in the urban life of Delhi [...], as his confessor, and he probably means to teach him the crookedness of his world that the youngster is going to enter, or has just entered.[18]

Ratan's authority over the boy is not then a moral issue (because, if things had to be judged under this perspective it would rather be the opposite), but it comes from his experience, from the lesson he himself has learned. As he declares, "Some facts of life, like drowned sailors, surface only with time. And as one grows older, these forgotten bits are clearer than what happened last year, or last week, or this morning"[19], hence his need to describe everything in detail. Both his mastery of the subject and his affection for the student are quite evident in another case. Still at the beginning, Ratan and his listener are discussing respect :

> To be respected. To be of use. Who has not wanted them? Yet how few manage it. Simple things like that. Things as basic to life as air and water. And so difficult to get!
>
> What? Or we do not know how to get them? Yes, perhaps we do not know how to get them. You might be right.

The discourse is, therefore, shaped according to the boy's ability to understand the focal matter. Ratan in fact knows very well "how to get them". At that juncture in the plot — we are still at the beginning — the listener/reader is still largely unaware of the ghosts which haunt and crowd the narrator's past. Hence, to contradict the youngster at this point may appear as a sterile prevarication.

Considered under this light, the narrator and his interlocutor may represent a wise man and his disciple. In such an occurrence, the structure of the novel would refer to the structure of a purana or to some of the Upanishads, where a dialogue between a sage and a/some pupil/s has the declared intention of teaching a moral lesson.

The choice to listen to a single voice of a dialogue obviously implies the use of a language which is directly based on oral discourse. Yet, its use is very different from the same technique in Raja Rao's *Kanthapura*, the other Indian novel with similar features; while Raja Rao chooses an uneducated brahmin widow to unfold the plot, Arun Joshi's narrator is a man whose ability and skills are not ordinary. In a very revealing self-analysis, after focussing upon his shortcomings, Ratan declares :

> In fairness to myself let me mention that I had certain qualities, skills rather, that were not to be found among clerks. Or even higher ranks, for that matter. I prepared notes, for example, that went right through to the highest levels without anyone in between having to change so much as an "i". And those notes were mostly on obscure or complicated issues, requiring integration of material from several sources. Normally, officers dread such cases for the fear that a slip-up on any one fact might lead to serious mistakes. You can imagine, therefore, how it lighted everyone's burden to have a man amidst their clerks who could take care of every angle.[20]

This kind of orality has, therefore, a higher register than that used by Rao's narrator because of the different nature of the two story-tellers. There are though some devices Arun Joshi adopts for a peculiar rendering of such a form which need closer analysis. The *incipit*, to start with, reveals the use of a realistic Indian English which one cannot miss. There is a limited choice of novels in Indian English fiction that may match this powerful characterization in only a few lines :

> Yes? The way to the grounds? Certainly. If you turn right in font of the temple and go up the street and take a bus at the crossing.

> Or, if you could wait a little I shall drop you. I go the same way. Can you wait? Good.[21]

In particular, the use of "yes" as an approaching formula, so widespread in the oral use of Indian English, drastically reduces the distance between narrator and interlocutor and it appears as a most original way of approaching a novel, too. The choice to start the narration abruptly, *in medias res*, as if the exigencies of the reader were the least cared of, vehemently draws the reader's attention to the unfolding of the plot. The beginning of each new chapter recording Ratan's voice halfway through his dialogue and insisting on a language deeply structured on orality, appears to be a major concern of the writer. Compare the following :

> Here you are! Almost the last.[22]
> Well, well, I did not know you were a National Cadet.[23]
> Yes, last Sunday I could not come.[24]
> Have I come up the hard way?[25]
> Yes, to begin with, I had been afraid. I was afraid that people would come to know.

The recurrent adoption of "yes" as a starting formula recalls one of James Joyce's use of it in *Ulysses* as a closure. Having due regard to the difference in scale and presentation, the comparison with the masterpiece of the Irish writer is not out of place. The father-son relationship between two characters, a somehow guilty man and a youngster who meet in a most accidental manner, is the first illuminating feature. Moreover, a "Dilli" Leopold Bloom, Ratan Rathor projects the past events of his life into an urban context, narrating as he does his autobiography while walking and driving through the streets of Delhi, while stopping at "the best tea-shop of the neighbourhood"[26], while watching military and religious parades. Yet, since Arun Joshi uses a language patterned on the inner dynamics of orality and as he renders half of a dialogue between two characters rather than an interior monologue, the stream of consciousness technique has to undergo some re-adjustments, lest it lack that immediate understanding which lies at the core of each pleasant conversation. For this reason, of all the senses, Arun Joshi makes an extensive use of sight in Ratan's narrations in order to meet both ends. The visual perception has the leading role while collecting together the various pieces of an acute memory. The first description of his Brigadier friend, coincise but essential, has such an exclusive focus on visual perception that it acquires a powerful motion-picture impact.

> The Brigadier had laughed at this. I can see him now. Head thrown back, handsome, scar across one cheek, memento of a previous war, sleeves rolled to the elbow, straight nose, even teeth. He was in uniform. He was sitting with his feet up on a table, long legs crossed at the ankles, staring into the cup of a yellow rose.[27]

And this is not the only example of the adoption of such a tecnique. Other similar cases, for instance, are those of the description of the old clerk[28] and that of the countryside around his own village[29], the last one, in particular, a long passage made out of a sequence of images not even connected by a single verb.

Another way of rendering the stream of consciousness technique inside a dialogue is that of mixing present and past into a intricate pattern so that reality and memory cannot be more distinctly separated. In the following passage, moreover, the author drastically reduces the difference between the interlocutor and the reader so that the two merge into one single person. Once more, the visual perception is focal :

> It gets late. See how the smoke descends, like mist; a black fog. In winter you can tell the hour by the density of the smog. The streets are emptying but soon they will be filled again, when the cinemas disgorge their hold. You live nearby? Perhaps I can walk with you a little distance even thought I really ought to go home. It has been almost a year since I walked these streets. There was a time last year when I came here often; especially to one particular square not far from here.
>
> There look at the houses, cliffs in the night. I am sure in daylight you have seen their true face : dilapidated, ugly, stairways soaked in beetle spit. But at night — ah, at night it is another matter. The night lends them a magic of its own. Yes, at night, for all

> their corruption and their dead, they come alive and there it was that I repaired so frequently during those weeks before the war.
>
> You see that unlit window above the empty doorway? I had a friend living there, a prince of the underworld, a man without a name. They called him the Sheikh. He is gone now, back to the garbage dumps that conceived him.

Therefore, this is not only the oral style of a character who talks at length, but it also renders a man walking and pointing at the various things he sees along his way. The images his eyes perceive — and that he soon puts into words — are the contemporary result of present vision and past sensations; hence, this poetical mood. There is another passage which reveals the peculiar use of this technique. Actually, it is not really a stream of consciousness as it is commonly considered; the language undergoes a sort of re-definement in order to stand a conversation. On the other hand, the writer reproduces the dynamics of the discourse imitating the itinerary a thought follows through the remote recesses of the mind; in this case the narration is not subject to any rule of logic, but rather to an irrational cause-effect route skipping from the sudden impulse of an emotion to the past memory of painful events which apparently have nothing in common. It is worth remembering that at this juncture in the narrative Arun Joshi places the epiphany of the novel. After a long period of careless selfishness, Ratan abruptly decides to undertake a sea-change. The revolution he talks about[30] starts from the very structure of this passage. The subject he describes at the beginning is the Brigadier.

> All at once, getting up abruptly, he started to pace the verandah. And I noticed then the strange wobble in his gait as though he were a ship on the high seas, a ship that had broken her rudder. His feet seemed to fall not on a straight line but at an angle so that every time he took a step he glided sideways until he reached a wall, turned about and glided back in the other direction. And all the while he continued to mutter under his breath. [...]

> I watched him with a sense of doom. And watching him I remembered the autumn evenings on an athletic field and in the growing dusk the cry of a nightingale. Believe, my friend, that was a rare, honest moment in my life. If I ever had been an honest man, a man deserving to walk upright, it was then. It was the second time in my life that I had felt the pain of another as my own, the first being the time when my father was shot. Yes, I had felt — and can still feel — I had felt that bullet in my chest; I, too, had spun around and, then, I had felt the second bullet in the hollow of my back. And standing thereby the glass window I felt as though it was not the Brigadier but I who was rocking through some dark dungeons of the world. And, you know, wading through this dark I did something that I had almost forgotten how to do : I prayed. [...]
>
> I said to my self : I shall be good. I shall not be greedy. I shall not be afraid. I shall be decent.[31]

Displacement, redemption, sentimentalism, rage, shame discomfiture, serenity : these are the elements which alternatively flavour a narration wisely structured on a most refined use of a technique which is always at the service of the mood of the moment. The result is that we have an X-ray vision of Ratan Rathor's soul, a character fighting against many violent inner forces at the same time, and with the unfortunate destiny of being possessed by a pride that forces him to win at all costs. The authenticity one perceives reading this novel is not such a strange factor, after all. Borrowing from his own characters (or should one say the other way round?), Arun Joshi surprised his interviewer when, after receiving the Sahitya Akademi Award in 1993 for *The Last Labyrinth*, he said about *The Apprentice* : "This novel still remains my favourite."[32]

REFERENCES

1. Pier Paolo Piciucco, "An Interview with Arun Joshi," *Journal of Indian Writing in English* 25. 1 and 2 (Jan.-July 1997) : 95.

2. V.V.N. Rajendra Prasad, "*The Apprentice* : Self as a Labyrinth, *The Novels of Arun Joshi*, ed. R.K. Dhawan (Delhi : Prestige Books, 1992) 212.

3. The majority of critics considers it "a monologue". Among them are : Joy Abraham, *op. cit.*, p. 210; Gopal Reddy, "*The Apprentice* : An Existential Study," *The Novels of Arun Joshi, op. cit.*, 219; O.P. Mathur, "Survival and Affirmation in Arun Joshi's Novels," *Modern Indian Fiction* (Delhi : Abhinav Publication, 1993) 130.
4. Vision and Technique in *The Apprentice, The Fictional World of Arun Joshi*, ed. R.K. Dhawan, (Delhi : Classical Publishing Company, 1986) 211.
5. Arun Joshi, *The Apprentice* (1974; Delhi : Orient Paperbacks, 1993) 58.
6. *The Apprentice* 142.
7. *The Apprentice* 98.
8. *The Apprentice* 98.
9. C.N. Srinath, "The Fiction of Arun Joshi," *Literary Landscape* (Delhi : Mittal Publication, 1986) 56-57.
10. *The Apprentice* 75.
11. *The Apprentice* 48.
12. *The Apprentice* 16.
13. *The Apprentice* 7.
14. *The Apprentice* 10.
15. *The Apprentice* 91.
16. *The Apprentice* 100.
17. *The Apprentice* 8.
18. T. Guruprasad, "The Lost Lonely Questers of Arun Joshi's Fiction," *The Fiction of Arun Joshi, op. cit.*, 100.
19. *The Apprentice* 50.
20. *The Apprentice* 35.
21. *The Apprentice* 5.
22. *The Apprentice* 6.
23. *The Apprentice* 9.
24. *The Apprentice* 13.
25. *The Apprentice* 40.
26. *The Apprentice* 6.
27. *The Apprentice* 14.
28. *The Apprentice* 37.
29. *The Apprentice* 17.
30. *The Apprentice* 142.
31. *The Apprentice* 100.
32. Puraby Benerjee, "A Winner's Secrets," *The Sunday Statesman*, 27 Feb. 1983.

4

The Concept of Humane Technology in Arun Joshi's *The Foreigner*

SHIVANI VATSA AND RASHMI GAUR

Arun Joshi has produced very compelling works in fiction. He has, in *The Foreigner*, very dexterously handled some thought-provoking, grave issues like rootlessness, detachment, frustration, quest for better alternative, identity, crisis and self-realization, highlighting our glorious cultural heritage and imperishable moral values. His reputation has been steadily rising since the publication of this very first novel.

In his second novel, *The Strange Case of Billy Biswas*, he presents the predicament of Billy in this absurd world. Billy, the protagonist discontented and disenchanted from the contemporary civilization flees from it and takes refuge in the tribal wilderness of central India. What the "phoney society"[1] fails to provide him is given by primitive life. Billy, as a matter of fact, does not endeavour to bring about the much needed change in the society. Sindi Oberoi, the protagonist in Arun Joshi's first novel, however, does not escape from the problems of the society. He comes back to the world and tries to succour the worker of the industry. He endeavours to develop a humane technology in the society for the better and healthy development of individual in this ostentatious and hypocritical world.

"Humane technology" is a ray of hope in the darkness of modern world. While technological innovations have an important place within the society, they also lead a precarious life. There is a growing antagonism between man and technology. Arun Joshi illustrates that "total industrialization" and "total automation"[2] result in the frustration that lead to various pathological states. The triumph of things over people leads to our spiritual alienation which results in the wholesale destruction of the personality. The word 'humane technology' refers to a technology that is kind and friendly to man, a technology that does not destroy the initiativeness of man in this urbanised world. The novels of Arun Joshi depict the urgent need of establishment of humane technology in our sordid civilization. *The Foreigner* illustrates the corrupting influence of technology on modern man. The modernization and industrialization is heading our civilization to a disaster. Modern man in contemporary society finds himself lonely, frustrated, dejected, secluded and almost alienated due to his detachment and non-involvement with his fellow-beings. Arun Joshi being himself connected with the industries and technology takes up this theme beautifully and emphatically. Arun Joshi's novel are the revelation of human predicament in an indifferent and inscrutable universe. The present society is full of exploitations. There is only chaos, confusion and anarchy in social life. Men do not realize their duty and responsibility towards others. The present decadence is the result of technological developments which have highly intensified the struggle of existence leading "to the detriment of the free development of the individuals"[3]. The revolution in technology affects man's innerself, the very structure of his personality, as well as the organisation and character of human activity. Arun Joshi was pained to see the chaotic conditions of the society. He, therefore, took into his hand the task of providing a solution to the society, to escape from the vicious circle of rapid industrialization. Thus, through the struggles of his protagonists he aims to achieve a good society and happy and joyful individuals.

In view of Arun Joshi the world today has become very materialistic, so much so that the higher values of life seem to have gone to the background. In the present world, material considerations dominate man's life. The result is that there is chaos and confusions in the life of individuals. Distrust, treachery, exploitation. etc., dominate the present world. There is an all-round attempt to invent machines and control nature to the advantage of man, and scientists have largely succeeded in their task. All this development of science and technology has not brought peace to the human mind. Today the human beings are not happy and contented. We are inclined to hold that despite of all th..e developments modern man is not happy. Life has, today, become aimless sport to passions, social prejudices, and national antagonisms. Human virtues life fellow-feeling, love, sympathy, kindness etc. have disappeared altogether. *The Foreigner* reveals that this highly sophisticated dehumanized technology itself now produces some of our most vexatious problems. The urbanized environment stirs sharp emotions in each man — sadness, hate, frustration, hopelessness and utter dejection.

The Foreigner illustrates the traumatic influence of urbanization and industrialization on man. The protagonist of the novel, Sindi Oberoi is a restless and uprooted character in an inept and sordid world. This novel superficially, may seem to deal with the theme of East *Vs.* West or the East - West encounter but, as a matter of fact, *The Foreigner* is, in the main, the study of an uprooted young man living in the latter-half of the twentieth century who looks out concernedly for mooring and a meaning in his randomly drifting life. The novel takes us to the lower depths of human suffering and agony arising due to the rapid advancement of technology. Born of an English mother and an Indian father who died when Sindi was only four, he was brought up by his uncle in Kenya. He was educated in East Africa, London and America. Denied of parental love, at such a tender age, Sindi doesn't feel any love or affection towards his parents. Sindi had felt some kind of security when his uncle was alive, "after his death, the security was destroyed."[4] Denied of love, care, security and cultural roots, Sindi grows with a cleft in his personality and becomes a rootless, wandering alien. When Mr. Khemka wants to know how the death of his parents took place, his reply has a sting :

> "For the hundredth time I related the story of those strangers whose only reality was a couple of wrinkled and cracked photographs".[5]

Sindi is alienated from the whole apparatus of society. He calls himself "an uprooted youngman living in the latter-half of the twentieth century who had become detached from everything except himself"[6]. His predicament is clearly revealed in his dialogue with Mr. Khemka :

"But you atleast knew that. You had a clear-cut system of morality, a caste system that laid down all you had to do. You had a God; you had roots in the soil you lived upon. Look at me. I have no roots. I have no system of morality. How does it mean to me if you call me an immoral man. I have no reason to be one thing rather than another. You ask me why I am not ambitious. You ask me why I am not ambitious; well I have no reason to be. Come to think of it I don't even have a reason to live"[7]

The Foreigner relates the story of its narrator, who reflects helplessly on his meaningless part and is apprehensive of his equally meaningless future. He feels uprooted and lost like a 'foreigner anywhere'[8] and endeavour all through his life not to get involved with anybody or anything until he at last gets to know what detachment actually means. Sindi believed in detachment from world and its affair which resulted in his loneliness : "I had to admit to myself that I was a lonely man"[9]. His non-involvement, apathy, loneliness and strangeness make him distant and foreigner wherever he went.

June remarks on his "foreignness"[10] : "There is something strange about you, you know. Something distant. But I have a feeling you'd be a foreigner anywhere"[11]. Even Shiela during Sindis' visit to India, comes to the same conclusion, she says to Sindi : "You are still a foreigner. You don't belong here."[12] He himself muses over his foreignness :

"………. I wondered in what way, if any, did I belong to the world that roared beneath my apartment window. Somebody had begotten me without a purpose and so far I had lived without a purpose, unless you could call the search for peace a purpose. Perhaps I felt like that because I was a foreigner in America. But then, what difference would it have made if I had lived in Kenya or India or anywhere place for that matter? It seemed to me that I would still be a foreigner. My foreignness lay within me and I couldn't leave myself behind wherever I went……"[13]

Sindi resented the ultra-modern and mechanized society. He knew "that….. the abominable wheel of industrialization was grinding on inevitably"[14]. Conscious of the unceasing gyration of the "wheel of civilization"[15]. Sindi remarks on the nature of modern man to Mrs. Blyth when she brags about the longer life span of Americans :

"And what use have you made of your extra height and extra years? You carry heavier guns and have a longer time to make each other unhappy, that's all. Can you call that an achievement?".[16]

Sindi is aware of the destructive influence of rapid industrialization on man. The mechanized modern civilization razes the inner-self of man. Affectation, hypocrisy and artificiality have come in the wake of industrialization in our society. Arun Joshi highlights the class-consciousness and class-conflict in the novel. The novelist hints at the class-conflict by highlighting the contrast in the living standards of Mr. Khemka, the employer and Muthu, the employee. Sindi is awestruck on his first visit to Mr. Khemka's mansion :

"I looked .... At the richness of Mr. Khemkas' drawing room. This was no doubt Indias' affluent society. Plush carpets, low streamlined divans, invisible lighting, bell buttons in every corner, and sculpture".[17]

In contrast to the mansions of wealthy people are the slums of the poor-section of the society :

"The slums across the street, bundles of soggy humanity shuffled out of their huts and spread their miserable rags to dry. Full-breasted women, their thighs naked under wet saris, scurried back and forth like animals quarreling over small bits of tin. Naked children rolled in the filthy pools, squealing with delight"[18]

The mode of life and the set of values which Khemka and his friends follow makes Sindi sick. Sindi though labelled as an Indian, is an outsider, a stranger, a foreigner in India too. He is filled with disgust to know how Mr. Khemka and his tribe exploited needy people like Jain and Muthu so that their empire could grow and expand.

In spite of Sindis' most intimate and intense moments of passions with various girls in England, he cannot get entangled with anyone of them in marriage as he comes to the conclusion that, "Marriage was more often a lust for possession than anything else. People get married just as they bought new cars".[19] Sindi is threatened with the fear of the loss of his identity, by his contact with others. D.H. Lawrence's Paul Morel is also the same case. In his *Sons and Lovers*, Paul seeks to confirm his identity through his relationship with Miriam. He tries to maintain a safe distance between them. When Miriam turns out to be possessive, Paul feels his self is threatened. "I can only give you friendship — It's all I am capable of — It's a flaw in my make up."[20] Thus, "one should be able to detach oneself from the object of ones' love".[21] The false detachment of Sindi drives both June and Babu to death. "Sindis' fetish for detachment and his fear of causing pain to himself results in the death of his beloved June and his friend Babu."[22]

Witnessing the terrible consequence of detachment, Sindi decides to leave America and go to India :

"Like many of my breed, I believed erroneously that I could escape from a part of myself by hopping from one land marks to another".[23]

Sindi by just a flip of coin leaves from India and realizes that India is not better than America. Sindi finds America "a place for well-fed automations rushing about in automatic cars"[24] and much "too clean and optimistic and empty"[25]. Arun Joshi presents the hectic and mechanized life of America. Sindi notices the hypocrisy and artificiality of the modern society in America. Participants at the ball arranged by the International students Association pretend to be courteous. Even the strangers at the time of parting promises to meet again, knowing fully well that it would not be possible :

"Strangers partied on the doorsteps promising to meet again, knowing fully well they didn't mean it. It was the American way".[26]

Similar is his experience at the social parties at Mr. Khemkas' house. He finds parties to be a bit of hoax with people drinking acting and talking of money — doing nothing worthwhile:

> "Like all balls, the whole thing was quite a fraud. It was intended to bring foreigners in contact with Americans, but ail it ever achieved was animosity; every body ended up hating the Americans all the more."[27]

Sindi realizes that the two cultures : American and Indian can never meet or come together. He discovers both the civilizations to be destructive and tyrannical. The material prosperity and individualism rampant in both the civilizations make Sindi unhappy and fail to provide him a state of peace within and calm around. For

Babu, America is a dreamland of free sex and there is no use of coming to America if one is not to play around with girls. He is a typical Indian who declares :

> "I would never go back to India if I had the choice".[28]

But Sindi and June know better that Americans are not "very congenial towards foreigners"[29]. Arun Joshi explorers the cleavage, the prejudices and illusions of the East and the West, in this novel. Sindi soon comes to realize :

> "In truth it had only been a change of theatre from America . The show had remained unchanged".[30]

The people of India are like Americans in "squeezing happiness out of the mad world"[31] though they have a different way of doing it. Sindi after deciding his destination : "looked forward to visiting the land of ancestors with an interest had not felt before"[32]. Sindi feels himself to be a misfit in the ultra-modern society of Boston. But his foreign background makes him a misfit in the Indian society also. "You are still foreigner. You don't belong here"[33] are Shielas' remark to Sindi clearly indicating the extraneous nature of Sindi.

Man in modern society fails to perceive the true meaning of life, the essence of human existence. Scientific and technological advancement have let to the loss of moral values, customs and traditions of the society. This advancement has engulfed man in a tragic mess of rootlessness, loneliness and meaningless. The rapid growth of affluent society, the poverty and hunger of the masses, the deterioration of moral values, the tension between ensuring generations resulting from changing ethos make increasing and often disturbing demands on the individuals and lead to their predicament. Arun Joshi has tried to project, through Sindi, the dehumanizing impact of technology and highly industrialized modern civilization on individuals. Sindi is a quester who "wanted to know the meaning of life"[34]. The protagonist of the novel, Sindi Oberoi goes on hopping from one country to another because he finds his life meaningless and rootless and thus valueless and purposeless. Sindi "very soon tired of the classroom lectures"[35] in London continued his search for "meaning of life"[36]. He realizes the futility of human achievements and purposelessness of his life at the bare age of twenty-five when normally a young man is full of enthusiasm, energy and zest for life. He gives expression to his feelings thus :

"And yet all shores are alien when you don't belong anywhere. Twenty-fifth Christmas on the planet. Twenty-five years largely wasted in search of wrong things in wrong places. Twenty-five years gone in the search of peace and what did I have to show for achievement : a ten stone body that had to be fed four times a day; twenty-eight times a week. This was the sum of a lifetime of striving".[37]

Ursula in *Women in Love* ponders : "A life of barren routine, without inner meaning, without any real significance …. One could not bear any more of this shame of sordid routine and mechanical nullity … And all life was a rotary motion mechanized, cut off from reality"[38]. Sindi endeavour to find a meaning in the absurdity around him. Since he considers his life to be full of illusions, he is unable to find his roots anywhere in the world. He ruminators on the purposelessness of his life :

> "….. I was a foreigner in America. But then, what difference would it have made if I had lived in Kenya or India or anywhere place for that matter?"[39]

Arun Joshi in the novel delineates man's predicament particularly the feelings of loneliness and meaninglessness that have come as a result of worldly success, material prosperity and disintegration of all bonds of love and solidarity.

Muthu, an uneducated man teaches Sindi the distinction between detachment and involvement.

> 'Sometimes detachment lies in actually getting involved'.
> He spoke quietly, but his voice was firm with conviction".[40]

The struggle of Muthu to provide food and shelter to his own family and the family of his own brother, reveals to Sindi the real meaning of life which one finds sin developing, friendly, sympathetic understanding. The blurb of The Foreigner of the needs of the other person. Sindis' experiences in India in the beginning were obviously not much different from those in West. The show had continued and only the theatre had changed. Gradually Sindis' understanding deepens as he roots himself into the world of the miserable who live in rags. Human suffering awakens him from deep slumber to the real meaning of detachment and also purges him. After his meeting with Muthu, a major change is noticeable in Sindis' attitude towards the real pursuit of human life. When, after an income-tax raid, Mr. Khemka is undertrial and there are rumors of his firm being bought over by some other firm, Sindi decides to leave for Bombay. Muthu, on meeting Sindi, after his return, requests him to take over the office so that the poor workers of the factory are not retrenched.

> "Everybody seems so worried he can hardly do his own job, leave alone understanding what the problems are. Those who could get other jobs have already left. The rest of us spend the day wondering what we will do when the axe finally falls. Actually it is rather a pathetic situation".[41]

Sindi is once again unwilling to be involved with the matters of Mr. Khemka and his workers. When he expresses his unwillingness to be involved, Muthu replies :

"But it is not involvement, Sir. Sometimes detachment lies in actually getting involved."[42]

Sindi understands finally that detachment does not mean escape or alienation instead it means involvement, devotion and sacrifice. His quest for the meaning of life comes to an end and Sindi takes over the management of the imprisoned Mr. Khemka business and becomes fully devoted to his task at hand. He decides to carry the sinking ship ashore and to achieve his goal hurls himself headlong into the battle of survival which the workers of the factory could not have won without his help, co-operation and guidance. Now he calls himself 'Surrender' instead of 'Surindra' as he has learnt the secret of genuine detachment. He works day and night forgetting his self-interest for the benefit of the workers of factory. Sindis' decision to save the ruined business of Mr. Khemka and to infuse new life into it is heroic one. Sindi leaving his self-interest aside helps out all those employees who earn their familys' daily bread by working in that factory. Sindi is filled with the desire to serve others and this feeling reduces the loneliness, frustration and apathy in Sindi and it also creates the deepest feeling of happiness, joy and gladness of heart in him. The journey from America to India, though had been long, but Sindi ultimately reaches his destination. He attains the goal of peace within and without emanating from a meaningful existence and a sense of belonginess.

"Mr. Sindi Oberoi, a man totally alienated from his surroundings and society and even from his love, turns out to be the saviour of factory — workers"[43].

Rahul in *So Many Hunger*! written by Bhabani Bhattacharya, loves his works and his family but the sufferings of the people shake him and he is able to rise above his own needs to think of others, to think in others, to think in terms of his people and their humanity. He is able to shed his fear of suffering and loneliness :

"What happened to him as an individual did not matter. It only mattered what happened to his people."[44]

In the modern society, money is the highest of all values. There is a wide prosperity gap between the rich and the poor of the society. Wealth accumulated in the hands of few individuals exploited the masses and reduced them to poverty and servitude. Such a society is violent and oppressive. Mr. Ghosh, the income-tax officer while on his first contact with Sindi states about the revolution in the society that would bridge up all the gaps between different classes. He is of the opinion that : "It is only people like you, and Mr. Khemka who are holding back the revolution."[45] He also says : "India is working towards a new age. Mr. Oberoi," he said grandly, "An age in which each man will be equal to another."[46] Background with middle-class conventional values is driven to death by the glossy ways of America. The modern civilization devours all those who are not able to resist the pressures of industrialization.

Through *The Foreigner* Arun Joshi reveals to us his keen awareness and understanding of a deeper reality of our times. He depicts the presence of dissonance and despair among people with refined sensibility because of the pursuit of material possessions, individual identity and non-involvement. The search for meaningful existence ends when one achieves the state of happy co-existence and harmony with his fellow-beings. The novel portrays the protagonists' sense of anguish at the meaninglessness of the human condition. The central subject of Arun Joshi, the novelist, is the darkness of the soul which is the result of increased industrialization and mechanization in our lives. The protagonist is the lovely quester moving about in the absurd and meaningless world. The protagonist in the world of Arun Joshi is fluttering in dark night in the ruined city of the soul and attempts to find his way despite all the hindrances. Arun Joshi seems to present a solution to face the meaninglessness of life. He suggests that one can realize the essence of life by liberating the self from the clutches of cruel civilization and by paying due attention to the calls of the inner being. This is the only way of saving man from the purposelessness and degradation of the contemporary meaningless world. The detachment which Sindi so earnestly practices becomes a source of deeper agony to him. It is his detachment that is responsible for the tragedy of June and Babu. Before "the abominable wheel of industrialization"[47] Sindi feels driven "Like torn bits of paper on a windy day"[48]. The impact of rapid modernization accuring from industrialization and urbanization make increasing and often demanding demands on the individuals. The present society is deprived of ancient wisdom which made life meaningful and purposeful. The present man has shrunk in spirit and is domed to live in confusion, frustration, disintegration, disillusionment and meaninglessness. Arun Joshi has tried to project through the experiences of his protagonist the terrifying dehumanizing impact of urbanized and highly industrialized modern civilization on the individuals. As the processes of industrialization and urbanization gather momentum, the issues of ethics, values and social responsibility becomes more and more crucial and come to the fore. The affluent and economically well-off people has made the whole system corrupt and dishonest;

"I said why didn't you bribe them"

and

"I did it because everybody does it. You can't run a business these days without doing these things".[49]

Arun Joshi unravels the facets of crisis in modern man's life. He gives a fictive form to the chaos and confusion in the minds of contemporary men and then correlates it to human condition. This novels is both a chronicle of chaos and a mode of quest. Arun Joshi through his protagonists projects the impact of modern urbanized civilization on individuals. D.H. Lawrence too has dealt with the harmful effect of industrialization on men. In his novels like *Sons and Lovers*, he through his character, Annable scorns at the modern civilization : "All civilization was the painted fungus of rottenness"[50]. But, since science and technology in the age of D.H. Lawrence had not progressed so much, he didn't gave a full picture of dehumanizing impact of industrialization on men.

Industrialization, is a curse for mankind. The present distress is undoubtedly insufferable. Selfishness dominates to one another. The supreme consideration of Arun Joshi is man. The machines should not tend to make atrophied the limbs of man. The mad rush for wealth must cease. Modern civilization is by and large materialistic, hedonistic and economically speaking money and profit-oriented. The present day unrest is due mainly to our laying too much emphasis on matter and material comforts to the complete neglect of moral progress. The blind use of machines and technological development have destroyed our value system.

The novels of Arun Joshi describe that the problems which were created by the last few decades of rapid technological developments have proved that the world has made a fetish of technology. What was once an instrument in man's hand is fast reducing man into an instrument and threatening its survival. The craze for higher standards of living and technological progress *per se* are speeding up the destruction of the natural world. Arun Joshi advocated that technology is for man and not man for technology. It, thus, must not become the master of man. He, therefore, advocated a "humane technology". The cure of all the evils and ills of modern society lies in the establishment of humane technology. It is only in and through the cultivation of humane technology that the salvation of mankind is possible. The ultimate goal of humane technology is the welfare of the entire human race.

Thus, according to Arun Joshi, the only solution available to control the dehumanizing impact of science and technology is to maintain an optimum balance between science and technology and ethics and human values. Man, though cannot completely refuse an industrialization as man will then die of lack of food and other basic amenities, but one can definitely keep the pace of industrialisation under control. Thus, what we require the most is the establishment of humane technology which would ensure the required development of industrialisation, and thus that would do no harm to whole mankind. Arun Joshi suggests a synthesis of tradition and modernity with a view of fashioning a culture which will be conducive to the development and progress of both the individual and the society.

REFERENCES

1. Arun Joshi, *The Strange Case of Billy Biswas* (New Delhi : Hind Pocket books, 1971), p. 185.
2. Valetina Ivasheva, *On the Threshold of 21st Century* (1978), p. 157.
3. Albert Einstein, *Ideas and Opinions* (Allahabad, Rupa Books, 1992), p. 15.
4. Arun Joshi, *The Foreigner* (New Delhi : Hind Pocket Books, 1968), p. 56.
5. *Ibid.*, p. 12.
6. *Ibid.*, p. 164.
7. *Ibid.*, p. 118.
8. *Ibid.*, p. 29.
9. *Ibid.*, p. 27.
10. *Ibid.*, p. 55.
11. *Ibid.*, p. 29.
12. *Ibid.*, p. 122.
13. *Ibid.*, p. 55.
14. *Ibid.*, p. 45.
15. *Ibid.*, p. 243.
16. *Ibid.*, p. 108.
17. *Ibid.*, p. 12.
18. *Ibid.*, p. 40.
19. *Ibid.*, p. 67.
20. D.H. Lawrence, *Sons and Lovers*, (New Delhi : Penguin books, 1948), p. 271.
21. Shyam M. Ansani, *A Study of Arun Joshi's Fiction* (the literary half yearly, Vol. xix, no. 2, July 1978).
22. Arun Joshi, *op. cit.*, p. 67.
23. *Ibid.*, p. 150.
24. *Ibid.*, p. 78.
25. *Ibid.*

26. *Ibid.*, p. 23.
27. *Ibid.*, p. 21.
28. *Ibid.*, p. 78.
29. *Ibid.*, p. 80.
30. *Ibid.*, p. 174.
31. *Ibid.*
32. *Ibid.*, p. 150.
33. *Ibid.*, p. 122.
34. *Ibid.*, p. 142.
35. *Ibid.*
36. *Ibid.*
37. *Ibid.*, p. 80.
38. D.H. Lawrence, *Women in Love* (New Delhi : Penguin books), p. 219.
39. Arun Joshi, *op. cit.*, p. 55.
40. *Ibid.*, p. 188.
41. *Ibid.*, p. 187.
42. *Ibid.*, p. 188.
43. A.N. Dwivedi, *The Novels of Arun Joshi — A Critical Study* (Papers on Indian Writing in English, Aman Prakashan,1991).
44. Bhabhani Bhattacharya, *So Many Hungers* (New Delhi : Vision books), p. 213.
45. Arun Joshi, *op. cit.*, p. 38.
46. *Ibid.*
47. *Ibid.*, p. 45.
48. *Ibid.*, p. 53.
49. *Ibid.*, p. 169.
50. D.H. Lawrence, *Sons and Lovers* (New Delhi, Penguin books, 1948).

5

Quest for Self in Arun Joshi's *The Strange Case of Billy Biswas*

URMIL

The Strange Case of Billy Biswas is a continuation of a development upon the first novel *The Foreigner*. Sindhi in *The Foreigner* and Billy Biswas in *The Strange Case of Billy Biswas* seem to be exploring things, trying to find out their own bearings and moorings. They are disillusioned and convinced that it would be pointless for them to try to participate in the indifferent anglicized social world of India. They are unable to relate themselves meaningfully to their surroundings and consequently with divided personalities they find themselves helpless in reconciling with themselves. Billy and Sindhi represent the predicament of the seeker — Who am I? Where am I from? and they oscillate between the modern and the primitive. The basic emphasis is on spiritual awakening and reintegration with the 'self'. Protagonists do not attain the stature of mythical heroes such as Lord Rama or Buddha. However, they undergo significant transformation in their response to life and relationship to other human beings. They are over-sensitive, have intensity of feelings and their mind is constantly under stress and pressure. Their major concern is with their inner world, the world of the soul and its source. They consciously give up the modern day world as they feel suffocated within their society. In the alien culture as well as their own society, they suffer, but this suffering is a purifying process, leading or at least pointing towards the promise of self-awakening rather than disillusionment. Their problem of communicating with the fellow beings disappears, because now they are seeking communion with the 'very centre of man's existence' rather than an assertion of their identity. They have a positive vision in the newly found world. What they seek is not specifically that component in an individuals personality which feels realized in the company of other selves, or which seeks relatedness with other similar selves. It is rather that part which responds to the beckoning of the very source of all beings wherefrom an individual self feels it has emanated.

Sindhi and Billy, after their exposure to Western cultural values become more conscious of their journey towards cosmic selves. On their return from a foreign land they are sad and spiritually broken, they venture forth from the world of common day into a region of the supernatural. There is a beginning of new existence as a 'conscious' being, in which state participation on social and individual plane cease to have any significance. The contrastive experience in two different socio-cultural environment adds a spark in their lives enabling them to rise above their own worldly self. Both Sindhi Oberoi and Billy Biswas act as foreigners to society as also to themselves and wander over the face of the earth in search of the essence of the 'source of existence.' Sindhi Oberoi declares : "My foreignness lay within me and I could not leave myself behind wherever I went." (Arun Joshi : *The Foreigner*, p. 65) (Orient Paperbacks, 1972). They want to resolve their alienation from within by tracing the meaning of existence from beginning to a real beginning. Sindhi's speech reflects their state of mind :

> "I didn't know where I would go or what the future held for me, but one thing was certain : my search had to continue. I had solved some of the questions my existence had posed for me; but many more resolved to be solved. I only wanted a place where I could experiment with myself." (*The Foreigner*, p. 185).

Sindhi and Billy Biswas get strength to resolve the inner conflict through the process of emotional involvement and ultimately they reach a stage where they have an intuitive perception of a supra-rational bonding with a certain mode of existence in harmony with the very centre of man's existence.

Arun Joshi portrays protagonists who are singularly individualistic but symbolize the characteristics of the modern age.

They explore the 'inner world' of modern man and the way in which the self tries to carve out a pattern to save itself from disintegration. Amid modern society they are aware of the dehumanizing effect of mechanisation and what they have lost. Most of them are highly educated abroad, their behaviour is incompatible with the laws of materialistic life around them. In their effort to revive from the sense of futility of life they explore the "dark mossy labyrinths of the soul that languish forever, hidden from the dazzling light of sun." (*The Strange Case of Billy Biswas*, p. 4). Whether being in the common day world or not, they find themselves lost within the unbounded prison of their own conscious minds. They are horrified at their isolation in a self-enclosed world that whirls continually around them. The outward journeys are symbolic of their quest for self-realisation. All of them yearn to transcend the materialistic region and arrive at a point which is a sort of salvation of the soul. In Arun Joshi's novels this awareness of the self is inspired by a confrontation with some crisis — the death of June for Sindhi in *The Foreigner*; the seduction of Rima Kaul for Billy in *The Strange Case of Billy Biswas*. The self is subjected to a groping and probing which is a great therapeutic process. The protagonists encounter all these labyrinths, but their groping in dark reaches an illumination of some sort. Their affirmations in different novels are personal but the eternal quest for self-realisation and spiritual fulfilment is distinctly one.

Sindhi Oberoi, the protagonist of *The Foreigner* is a rootless person in search of meaning in life. He was born in Kenya and brought up by an uncle due to the demise of his parents. He is a spiritual exile who feels lonely even in a crowded bar. He went to London, Boston and New Delhi, but a 'foreignness' affected him wherever he went. He found his soul alone in the darkness, divided against itself.

Sindhi runs away from commitment in love, determined as he is to remain detached after his escapades with Anna and Kathy. He thinks that attachment causes pain and he wants to escape it. Moreover he wants to withdraw from action because first he wants to know the purpose of action. Sindhi's philosophy of detachment and search for essence of life lead June and Babu to death. Their death cause an agonizing introspection in Sindhi. As he puts it :

> I was seized with the problem of once again putting together all that had happened to me and coming to grips with life. For twenty years I had moved whichever way life had led me. I had learnt much on the way. I had learnt to be detached from the world, but not from myself. That is when the fatal error was made that ultimately led to Babu's and then to June's death.
>
> (Arun Joshi, *The Foreigner*, p. 207)

Witnessing the terrible consequences of practising detachment in America, Sindhi comes to India and joins Khemka's firm as a manager. By constantly talking to Babu's sister Shiela and reading Babu's letter, he discovers the disastrous consequences of alienating the self from its roots. We find Sindhi a quester, with a schism in his soul. He realises that detachment is not enough to know the world objectively. His conversation with Shiela further confirms this :

> "You may be a wise man and I might admire you for your wisdom. But you forget how long it has taken you to get where you are. And all the destruction that you have caused in the process."
>
> She was right and I had nothing to say
>
> (pp. 230-31).

In his second novel *The Strange Case of Billy Biswas* Arun Joshi portrays how a man of extraordinary sensibilities is destroyed by the process of individuation. Novel seems to suggest that life's meaning doesn't lie in the world outside but within. The magnetic, mysterious forces of the universe took Billy to Bilasia's world where he felt free to express his own individual self unhampered by those ties which were limiting him while he was in the midst of upper crust of society. He staked his life in order to test the validity of some of his intuitions about life. He is driven to death by the mad, absurd world — when he tries to retrieve his soul from the labyrinth.

Billy Biswas in *The Strange Case of Billy Biswas* and Sindhi in *The Foreigner* try to liberate the self from normative demands of the money — worshipping social context and diagnose the malady

— the crookedness of the world. Both of them exercise their choice of freedom and dedicate themselves to the fulfilment of inner needs.

In *The Strange Case of Billy Biswas* Arun Joshi seems to be mediating between two conflicting forces — the primitive world and the modern anglicized Indian Upper Crust. The author reveals with great force the utter falsity of the anglicized Indian tradition of high culture and its resultant chaos. Man's feeling of alienation in contemporary civilised life gives an opportunity to the protagonist to muse over his life's purpose. He observes life objectively and finds himself an eternal outsider amid modern humanity. He finds something radical missing in life and tries to regain it.

The first part of the novel gives us glimpses of the restlessness of Billy's soul in the midst of the upper class Indian society, which is lost in the superficialities of life. The restlessness is not due to some negative attitude or error of judgement but due to the loss of traditional values in the materialistic pursuits by people in general. Romi, whom Billy meets in New York while searching for accommodation relates the story. It is an attempt to understand 'a man of...extraordinary obsessions' (p. 7). Both of them stay together during their higher studies and Romi noticed in their first meeting "the incongruity of his eyes...what went on in their dark depths" (p. 8). His father has been a justice of the Supreme Court of India and earlier he had been an ambassador to a European Country. Billy had his schooling in Europe. At present he is half way through his Ph.D. in anthropology, although his father thinks that his son is doing engineering. Billy explains his fascination for anthropology to Romi : "All I want to do in life is visit the places they describe, meet the people who live there, find out...the aboriginalness of the world" (p. 10). In fact it was around his interest in the primitive man that his entire life had been organised (p. 10). He stays at Harlem in New York though he could afford to live at some better place. But it is a natural choice for Billy because he feels that it was 'the most human place he could find' (p. 5). White America is much too civilised for him (p. 5). Romi's host describes him as an 'Engineer, anthropologist, anarchist....and thoroughly, crazy, even by Indian standards' (p. 5). He is a rare, man who has 'poise without pose' (p. 7). Most people who met him considered him a light-hearted good sport, but his eyes which were the dominating feature of his face never lost their deep sombre look. Tuula Lindgren, the Swedish girl, doing an advance course in psychiatric social work and Romi are the two persons who understand the dilemma of Billy's life. Romi feels : "What happened to Billy was, perhaps, inevitable" (p. 8). He could not have behaved otherwise. It is his vision of life which persuades him to search for 'the tenuous thread of existence to its bitter end' (p. 8). Tuula is a Swedish girl yet her values are centred around the vitalizing force of this life which brings her closer to Billy. She observes the spiritual degeneration in society objectively and knows how to encounter this utter confusion. She is a sensitive girl and understands the reasons and impacts of hallucinations in Billy's life. She knows 'what went on in the dark, inscrutable, unsmiling eyes of Billy Biswas' (p. 15). She is the first person Billy meets who has total disregard for money and treats it as 'a whole lot of paper' (p. 175). She is humane and believes in the Hindu philosophy of life. According to Tuula, once the basic needs for survival are fulfilled man should 'contribute as much to the society as you can' (p. 174). But what attracted Billy is Tuula's belief that the search for truth is a lonely business : "...you had to be prepared to go it alone if you really wanted to be honest to yourself" (p. 175). His choice of books, music, places reflects his deep interest for the primitive life. When a car driver splashed mud on Tuula Lindgren, Billy called him a 'Bastard' — an expression which he later uses for the civilised society. There is an inherent protest against mechanised, dehumanised civilised world where no one has any concern for others. Throughout the first section Arun Joshi gives a view of the rich inner recesses of Billy Biswas's world. Another evidence of primeval longing in Billy is seen in the 'music session' — he has at a party in George's apartment :

> 'Billy's session — for that was how it came to be known subsequently — lasted for nearly a quarter of an hour. I am certain it was nothing very skilful or sophisticated from the viewpoint of music. What it had, I think, was a mesmeric pull that held us by its sheer vitality. Little package of sound detonated in the smoke-filled air in quick succession, falling in one

> rhythm or another, creating patterns of sound that deep down I knew were not merely that but carried a more fundamental message although what it was I, or Billy for that matter, could not have said' (p. 17).

At such moments Billy goes for a 'long and difficult journey.' Billy explains to Romi how he often had hallucinations : "It would be like a great blinding flash during which I would be totally unaware of anything else. And invariably it left me with the old depressing feeling that something had gone wrong with my life. I wasn't where I belonged" (p. 179). Tuula is able to see the danger awaiting Billy on his return to India when she says that his well-connected family 'may be part of the difficulty, the difficulty in what he wants to do' (p. 18). Tuula is able to perceive that mysterious urge in him. She tells Romi, 'Billy feels something inside him but he is not yet sure.' She calls it 'A great force unkraft...a primitive force. He is afraid of it. But is very strong in him, much stronger than in, you or me. It can explode any time' (p. 19). She finds him "obsessed with a latent quest" (p. 176). Tuula believes that the conflict is between the primitive and the civilised but according to Arun Joshi it is a recurring conflict of "an essentially Hindu mind" (Reply to M.R. Dua). Billy tries to come out of alienation by participating in life with Tuula and Romi. During one of the conversations with Billy Romi observed that they were 'revealing not only the mind of the speaker but also the dark unknowable layers of the mysterious world that surrounded us' (p. 22). Talking about his glimpse of the other side Billy tells Romi : 'Most of us are aware only of the side on which we are born, but there is always the other side, the valley beyond the hills, the hills beyond the valley' (pp. 14-15). This other side concerns the primitive life untouched by the sophistication of the civilised world. He wants to penetrate deep into human life. He longs for integration with 'Reality' which may be termed as totality of 'Nature', nature here not in the physical sense alone but something at the level of which man's very being is seen in its quint essential, devoid of all external frills.

Billy stayed in America for long but does not 'suffer much, except for passing spells of loneliness, from that alienation that many other Indians seemed to be burdened with' (p. 21). He has the advantage of shared background. He is not bothered about cultural alienation; what teases him is the superficial reality of life. Although averse to the civilised world yet 'In the midst of an irregular and impromptu existence he maintains a steady progress in anthropology' (p. 20). The strong streak of primitivism is always present in Billy, he is more interested in far-away places and he wants to have a glimpse of 'fascinating societies' that exist in India (p. 10).

On his return to India he is appointed lecturer in Anthropology at Delhi University. Billy does not find the phoney, consumerism-ridden world of Delhi much different from the American materialistic society. Here also he feels like 'a visitor from the wilderness to the marts of the big city' (p. 92). He reflects :

> I see a roomful of finely dressed men and women seated on downy sofas and while I am looking at them under my very nose, they turn into a kennel of dogs yawning (their large teeth showing) or snuggling against each other or holding whisky glasses in their furred paws. I sometimes wonder whether civilisation is anything more than the making and spending of money. What else does the civilised man do? (p. 92).

Billy Biswas does not enjoy his role and finds it difficult to get used to the workings of his job and place. For him life in such an oppressive atmosphere has become a bleak business and he does not see a way out as to how he should crush the uneasiness of his mind. The people he meets here are nothing more than apes mimicking the forsaken ideas of West. Billy's predicament results from the confusion of values in civilised society. There is a wide gap between him and the modern Delhi society because 'beneath the shared facade of society, there was little contact between his world and theirs' (p. 59). To put a check on his 'imaginary running away' (p. 129) he marries a Bengali girl named Meena Chaterjee. At that time he finds no better girl than Meena. Moreover Billy admits : "What with being an Indian and having been brought in a close-knit family, the only thing I could think of was to get married" (p. 180). Perhaps Billy thinks that his marriage is like 'taking out an insurance on normalcy' (p. 180). He expected Meena to help him to put a check on hallucinations but he was greatly mistaken as it was a marriage between 'uneven minds'. "The game

I had been playing was the stupidest gamble one could think of. It was lost even before I had put up the stakes" (p. 180). He could not have imagined that one can be isolated from the other while staying so close. Inspite of being married Billy was essentially lonely as he could not feel free to be mentally independent and share his natural feelings with his wife. Even his wife didn't try to draw him out of and away from his imaginary self. She could not animate his tormented soul.

Billy's interest in anthropology gives him an opportunity to look at supernatural things, social facts from a different angle. For example, Billy defends before his father child-sacrifice by a clerk, he says :

> The point, however is this : Is it possible for an ordinary person — a government clerk, let us say — to receive a message from a goddess and, having received one, to pass into another world, not for an hour or a day but for a week, a month, one whole year, at the end of which he may return to his normal state. If this happens, as it seems to have happened in this case, what is to be the attitude of the society, of the law, if you please? (p. 49).

He asserts that these laws are made for this world only. A person operating under the laws of the different world should be judged according to the laws of the respective tribal world. When his father strongly disapproves of his theory, Billy says, 'It is only after it happens to oneself that one comes to believe....All I am saying is that there are worlds at the periphery of this one, above it and below it, and around it, of which we know nothing until we are in them' (pp. 50-51). Romi once again observes Billy's obsessive interest in the supernatural element. He avers : Billy's interest is in the supra-rational, mystic forces, his awareness of the limited jurisdiction of the scientifico-rational civilization — much more in heaven than you can dream of. He believes that the tribal world is in tune with its own norms and that it should not be judged by yardsticks of our own world.

Billy's marriage proves to be an ill-fated decision taken in a hurry as their life turns into the 'most precarious of battle fields'

(p. 77). He is unhappily married. He and his wife both are temperamentally poles apart. Meena, a product of the phoney society, has no idea of human suffering (p. 183). She fails to 'communicate' with Billy. She does not try to understand what troubles him inwardly, rather she becomes resentful whenever he tries to speak out his mind. She admits, 'Perhaps I just don't understand him as a wife should' (p. 72). To betray his loneliness, he had married Meena but now he is an uncared for person. Billy feels that he has been caught in a cobweb. He understands that he can overcome his alienation only through true, spiritual love. Meena's presence augmented his agony as he sees offensive contrasts stronger than ever before. Meena is only a representative of the erosion of values of the times. His last refuge failed him miserably. Marital incompatibility between Billy and Meena is the result of their commitment to different creeds and inability to appreciate and accommodate the other view point.

This incompatibility exacerbates Billy's growing disenchantment with this world. He suffers from dislocation and a sense of isolation. This listlessness had its impact on his physical appearance also. This is amply borne out in Romi's impressions. 'He seemed duller than most dull men that I usually met. It was virtually impossible to keep the conversation going.... It was as though some part of him had gone on strike.... Gone was the staggering intelligence, the spectroscopic interests, the sense of humour...the Billy Biswas I had known was finished, snuffed out like a candle left in the rain (p. 66).

Billy seeks a world uncontaminated by hypocrisy and selfishness. But the irony of fate is, he is at the centre of it. Meena Chatterjee's father who bewails the tragic deterioration of standard in Indian Civil Service is "the bloody old phoney", according to Billy. He performs his duty towards the so called civilised world like an automation. He is somewhere else. The society of Delhi is too much for him to be borne any more. He tells Romi :

> 'What got me was the superficiality, the sense of values. I don't think all city societies are as shallow as ours.... Artistically, they were dry as dust. Intellectually, they could not better than mechanically

> mouth ideas that the West abandoned a generation ago.... All that was left was loud mouthed women and men in three piece suits, dreaming their little adulteries' (pp. 176-77).

He considers himself a misfit, misplaced and does not enjoy the role he has earned for himself by virtue of his qualifications. He finds happiness neither in family nor in teaching. He seems to be misbegotten in a world which he does not seem to fit in. He does not have to be alone to be lonely. In fact, the most shocking experience of loneliness comes to him when he is in the midst of many. He is dissatisfied with the modern civilised culture, its standards and its mores which are perennially being imposed by its corrupt agents on creatures aching with listlessness. Billy himself explains to his friend Romi, the significance of dreams and psychic disturbances when as a collector he visits a hamlet ravaged by a terrible drought (p. 110).

The modern civilised society had its corrupting effect on Billy as well. He feels himself 'pinned down there, like a dead butterfly' (p. 43). He starts, to whine and to lie and sham. He starts to behave in a manner that in other men he had always despised. It is during this degeneration he seduces Rima Kaul. Billy is aware of the fraudulent nature of this relationship on his part and knows that he does not intend such a thing. Billy asks himself whether he belongs to the category which has this self-image. He is seeking something else. He feels horrified at his behaviour.

> 'It gradually dawned on me that a tremendous corrupting force was working on me. It was as though my soul were taking revenge on me for having denied it for so long that other thing that it had been clamouring for.' "Here you swine, if you haven't the guts to break away from this filth, well than, I am going to wallow in it until it makes you sick" (p. 187).

Seduction of Rima Kaul is the last warning signal to Billy which gives him a preview of the corrupting force which awaits him if he continues to defy what his soul longed for. His longing for his spiritual being can be traced to a very young age of fourteen when he feels concerned with the eternal questions like "Who was I? Where had I come from? Where was I going?" (p. 120). The same quest forces him to accompany a chauffeur in a village near Bhubaneshwar (p. 122).

Billy realises that all his efforts to integrate with society are futile, these are simply enhancing his restlessness. He listens to his inner self. Now he knows that Meena has failed to bring him out of the hallucinations. He tries to find his identity in Meena but fails. "I tried very hard to communicate with her" (p. 183). The tricks that work on others will not work for Billy. Marriage is seemingly a heroic act into which Billy has been shamed. After marriage what is still lacking is a sense of the unity of existence. Refined feeling ultimately rejects what initially appears likable. A deeper insight is lacking in Billy at the moment of decision, therefore, the happiness or solace he seeks betrays him. The experience realised by keen effort may be pleasurable for a moment but turns sour in its later consequences. The urge to live like a man in a primitive world has become stronger. To calm his frenzy he takes to anthropological expeditions.

During one of his anthropological expeditions along with his students he goes to Maikala Hills near Bhubaneshwar. Here he feels that he belongs to the primitive jungles rather than to the cities. 'The curious feeling trails me everywhere that I am a visitor from the wilderness to the marts of the big city and not the other way round' (p. 92). His otherself has grown stronger and he realises that he has been running after illusory appearances. To Romi's question, "But, don't you think you had responsibilities towards her, towards your son?" Billy's answer is, "I had greater responsibilities towards my soul." He decides to participate in a reality which in itself is the truth, namely his 'true being.' He transcends the mind, and once he is beyond the mind all his problems look as if they are somebody else's problems. Billy Biswas wants to detach himself from the illusory situation as he has experienced his freedom in anguish. There was no method by which he could hope permanently to establish a community of ends with other human beings, since he was locked in inevitable conflicts with others. The only remaining option was to choose his freedom. Billy all of a sudden disappears from the face of the earth into the sal forests. The whole area is combed for a year to trace him but the efforts proved futile. People believe that he has been killed by a man-eater. This disappearance from the civilised world is the termination of the pseudo self and an initiation into the deep, mysterious, real primitive world. He attains a state of watcher on the hills and all the problems are in the valleys. He leaves the civilised society because he is conscious that staying in it will yield evil consequences. The relaxed manner in which Billy departs from the phoney world shows his acceptance of the verdict of his state, and he magnificently straddled the gap between knowing and being. Billy withdraws from trivialities of life in the sophisticated society, which fails to sustain him and fulfil his urge for a meaningful life. This withdrawal is for the realization of his true identity and for integration with the vital forces of nature that will lead him to higher plane of experience. It is an effort to integrate with the real primitive self. In a way his authentic essence has the first opportunity to come into its full glory, into its absolute splendour. Billy Biswas is determined to carve out his own destiny.

The night he saw the tribal dance he had the premonition that it might not be possible for him to go back. Even as a boy he had been deeply concerned with the problem of his identity, "Who was I? Where had I come from? Where was I going? (p. 120). Amid the dance and liquor he realises the edifice of his past being chiselled away and a new primitive self come to the force. Even if the whole world dislikes it, if his conscience approves of it, he should indulge in it. He realises that it is wise to accept the life of which he dreamt regularly rather than continuously running away from life in search of the real meaning of life. He laments why he 'had been afraid, afraid and foolish, squandering the priceless treasure of his life on that hoop, of tinsel that passed for civilisation' (p. 139). Billy Biswas looks into future with his insight and instinct that tells him what to follow and what to avoid. It is these flushes of vision that lead him to seek suitable spiritual companion. He believed :

> 'If anyone had a clue to it (real self) it was only the adivasis who carried about their knowledge in silence, locked behind their dark inscrutable faces (p. 122).

The strong questing will has found its object; Bilasia and forest as his world. He underwent a metamorphosis and the real self now says :

> 'Come, come, come, come. Why do you want to go back? This is all there is on earth. This and the woman waiting for you in the little hut at the bottom of a hill. You thought New York was real. You thought New Delhi was your destination. How mistaken you have been! Mistaken and misled. Come now, come. Take us. Take us until you have had your fill. It is we who are the inheritors of the cosmic night' (p. 119).

Billy responds to the call and becomes one of the primitive people to find not only his roots but also identity. Once he is in forest, he is obliged to take the inhabitants as one vast family, of which he is a potent member, God's vehicle. The civilised world called him a rebel while tribals considered him as their friend as he cured Dhania's niece Bilasia.

When Billy sees the primitive girl Bilasia, his frenzied search is calmed. He finds his fulfilment in the love of Bilasia 'the essence of that primitive force that had called me, night after night, year after year' (p. 140). His love which had remained unspelt and inarticulate so far, now blows with the wild breeze. The meeting with Bilasia in Dhunia's hut on the night prior to his disappearance brought about a changc in him : "It was as though, during that half hour, it was not Bilasia I had been waiting for but my future, my past, indeed the very purpose of my life" (p. 111). Bilasia helped him to discover 'that bit of himself that he has searched for all his life and without which his life is nothing more than the poor reflection of a million others' (p. 140). His state of consciousness can be aptly described by a few lines in Wordsworth's Tintern Abbey :

> ...that serene and blessed mood
> In which the affections gently lead us on,
> Until the breath of this corporeal frame
> And even the motion of our human blood
> Almost suspended, we are laid asleep
> In body and become a living soul;

He feels that layers of superficiality were pealed off until nothing but his primitive self was left. 'Or, rather, quite suddenly and unaccountably I had ceased to resist what was the real me. All that I had been confusedly driving towards all my life had been crystallized.... I had changed. I knew that' (p. 114). In striving for growth, he identifies his real being with the germinal higher part of himself. He becomes conscious that this higher is continuous with a MORE (God) of the same quality and which he would keep in working touch with to save himself. This is the first instance of recognition of his individuality; what he had sought all his life, the realization of the 'being' in him. Now there is a gleam of hope. A disturbing knowledge dawned on him : 'Something has gone wrong with my life. This is where I belong. This is what I have always dreamt of (p. 123).

Billy's quest for self begins and he knows that he will be able to peep into dark cells of his soul by fleeing from the suffocating modern civilised society. A sort of precipitation occurred of what might be called insights or dreams. The tribal's dedication to the deity and their deep and overpowering love for him becomes the driving force and code of his activities. He finds a world where he is related to it through love and not through submission or dominance. It is a marriage of loving souls where love finds its consummate fulfilment far removed from the sanctimonious bonds of wedlock. This is a state of consciousness where Billy's identity merges into the cosmic identity. It is his love for the tribals and love in return from them which gives him a feeling of rootedness, belongingness. He eats their kind of food, speaks their language and wears their kind of dress. He experiences their joys and sorrows, living their beliefs and the tribal people soon adore him as their 'Mahaprasada'. He becomes as he himself thinks, 'some sort of a priest' (p. 189). He feels happy in the forest not because of money, position or a job but because of 'the earth, the forest, the rainbows, the liquor from the mahua, an occasional feast, a lot of dancing and love making, and more than anything else, no ambition, none at all" (p. 146). His embrace of primitive life is a part of the maturation of his being. Now he begins to realize his own self. When he finds his real self among the forest people, he is a different being, refuses to do anything with the modern civilised world. In rejecting modern society he rejected all wrong self-images to recognize his true self. His acceptance of the deaths of Rima Kaul and his mother with calmness reflects his maturation. Billy's calm acceptance of death is a sign of his living in close proximity with Nature where life and death are natural routine events, imbued with a meaning which people outside don't understand. He has stripped the old ties and is in the world of Bilasia.

For Bilasia money is nothing more than paper and she refuses to accept it in place of Billy. Billy understands that this is the place where he belongs, in a manner he has been released from the insolubility of the Indian upper crust. That happiness which may be like poison at first but becomes nectar at the end, which springs from a clear understanding of the self, is divinity. The self here achieves growth by self-discipline. Becoming a primitive is a means to seek something else,

> "What is that?"
>
> He seemed to be thinking.
>
> "God?" I prompted.
>
> "There, there, old chap, that is
> too big a world."
>
> "Something like that?"
>
> "Yes, something like that." (p. 187)

By becoming a tribal himself he knows that it is only in this world he can understand the ultimate motive of life.

Billy seeks something divine and 'Divine' he himself becomes — he is accepted as the king by the tribals. Different factors point to his magical powers. As soon as he arrived in their world Chandtola came to life, it started glowing after a long time; tigers run away at his sight, he can revive a dead man; He is believed to be the mythical sculptor king who ruled over the region thousands of years ago. It is the call of Chandtola 'just so that he may know who he was' that brought Billy to the primitive world. Billy's primitive love Bilasia helps him to integrate with the primordial force which didn't accept the temple as her abode earlier. Now after the union with the divine the devi had taken abode in Chandtola.

Bilasia is a manifestation of the divine force and Romi says about her :

> "What was Bilasia? What is the playful effervescence of mountain stream? What is sunlight filtering through a glade? What is the thunder of a volcano or the hardness of granite?.... I had the distinct, if somewhat confused, feeling that I was facing not merely a human being but also the embodiment of that primal and invulnerable force that had ruled these hills, perhaps this earth, since time began and that, our proud claims to the contrary, still lay in wait for us not far from the doorstep of our air conditioned rooms' (pp. 223-24).

Bilasia is an integral part of nature and an embodiment of the primitive world and it is she who helped Billy to replace his restlessness with 'Divine' serenity. The opaque became transparent and revealed spirit in its depth. She helped him lose all sense of bondage to the past, and with the loss of that bondage he is freed from the phoney world. It is a joyous and liberating moment for him. The insight he gained is from his 'inner being' and not from someone outside. Bilasia can be compared to Tuula Lindgren who exerts a great influence during Billy's stay in New York. She is the first person whom Billy meets and finds devoid of superficiality. Tuula understands his mind and suggests to him to keep a check on his hallucinations, while Bilasia helped him win over hallucinations and see reality. Whatever appeared to be happening in the dream, at all times, was wholly created in Bilasia's world. He thus realises on awakening that there was complete one-ness permeating and encompassing Bilasia's world, and all the activities and attributes were essentially the same from the beginning to the end : And with this realisation, there comes to him a glorious and complete liberation from the sufferings, the ups and downs, that he had been suffering in the state of dream. With the removal of dream illusion and ignorance, and direct knowledge of his real nature and self, he regains his basic and natural equipoise and peace. He views the world and all the creatures from a completely changed and revolutionised standpoint.

Arun Joshi introduces a mythical concept of "matra" in the novel. According to the Hindu tradition if somebody tries to overstep his "matra", he is punished for it. If Billy knows that he is a divine being and possess magical powers, he will lose his powers. Dhunia says :

> 'those who must not will hear of it, and Billy Bhai will lose his powers' (p. 157).

Strangely enough it proved to be true. As soon as Billy comes out of the confines of the primitive world, things began to go wrong. Romi discusses with Billy his magical powers. Once during these discussions, a shadow distracted him, taking him entirely in its embrace. It seemed to have come out of the temple and say 'There are things that the like of you may never know. There are circles within circles and worlds within worlds. Beware where you enter' (p. 190). Romi observes the divine force in Billy as he cures his wife Situ of a painful migraine and predicts rains when there is no sign of rain. Romi, a part of modern society becomes an instrument in the final tragedy of Billy. Romi's wife Situ compels him to divulge the secrets and passes on the information to Billy's father and Meena. For Billy's father and Meena his disappearance is still a 'childish escapade.' They put tremendous emotional and official pressure on him to reveal Billy's whereabouts. Romi, however understands their incomprehensibility :

> 'They were only the representatives of a society which, in its middle-class mediocrity, bracketed men like Billy with irresponsible fools and common criminals and considered it their duty to prevent them from seeking such meagre fulfilment of their destiny as their tortured lives allowed' (pp. 231-32).

Romi refused to deceive Billy's confidence in him as Billy had said, "If they ever get hold of me, they will not leave me alone. And you know what havoc it will play with my life here" (p. 205). Romi warned that something serious would happen if they persisted in that but the entire government machinery of the organised society is put into force to retrieve Billy. Romi had forgotten Mr. Biswas's advice, 'Don't ever quarrel with your boss, whatever the provocation... secondly, never let the police get an upper hand in time of crisis. Remember these and you will never have trouble' (pp. 51-52). It was irony of fate that this was precisely what Mr. Biswas had managed to achieve. The tribal world joined together to face the encounter but failed and the tragedy finally struck. Billy spears down a police constable and is shot dead.

> 'Billy,' I cried, 'Billy.' He opened his fast gazing eyes for a moment and appeared to look at me. 'You bastards', he said hoarsely. Then he died (p. 231).

Billy in a way finds his self in the primitive world and his search is a conscious search. He thinks that a change could be brought about in society through Romi. He forgets that civilized society would be as it had been. Billy cannot have existed simultaneously in two worlds. He has to severe his links. Again, his friend Romi tries to save him out of the tribal world which ultimately leads to destruction. Primitive world has its own boundaries which you have to honour. Symbol of comfort in one world is not the same in the other world. For the representatives of modern society like Meena, Billy's father, Billy is somebody being caught hold of by the tribal world and the man needs to be saved. This clash between modern day world and somebody who wants to make a change in it prevails till the end. That the protagonist is killed in the end reflects the indifference of the civilised society.

Juxtaposing Billy's quest for self with that of Raju and Rosie in R.K. Narayan's *The Guide* offers interesting insights into the two protagonists' endeavour. R.K. Narayan in *The Guide* and Arun Joshi in *The Strange Case of Billy Biswas* have dealt with the quest for self from different angles. In *The Guide*, Raju, the protagonist is placed in a dilemma to eke out his maturity the hard way. He seeks self-realisation in the traditional Indian way by seeking *nirvana*. In Billy there is a primitive, mystic force at work which instils in him a desire to join the tribal world. Billy is aware of this secular force since his childhood; when for the very first time he visited the tribal world. Both Raju and Billy are seekers of an abstract reality. Billy is aware of the divine force in him and he withdraws from the modern world in order to preserve his rich inward life, a renunciation to preserve his real self. While Raju loses the innocence of a Malgudi boy and degenerates into wickedness, playing roles such as that of a new businessman, a guide, Rosie's lover and finally the swami, it is his last role, that of a swami which transforms itself into reality. The influence of the modern age had alienated Raju from his real self and had made him egocentric. His life had gone to pieces because of the love of the lime-light. Here Narayan shows how folly can be turned into human achievement; Raju like any ordinary man has potential for the angelic as well as the satanic and after satiating his gross hungers, Raju is finally guided to his goal. The tribals in *The Strange_Case of Billy Biswas* and the villagers in *The Guide* know that it is the abstract reality which speaks through Billy and Raju respectively. In Raju's life there is a discontentment which ultimately leads him to a position where he undertakes the quest for reality. Billy is aware of this force and leaves the marts of the city intentionally. Here a force in which pre-civilised society believed in is working on Billy. Raju is unaware of the abstract force, therefore, chance plays its role. He is ultimately brought to a situation where he cannot but follow the straight and narrow path. An intuitive contact has developed between the character and the supra-human force outside.

For years Raju had moved whichever way life had led him. He had learnt much on the way. The external trappings of a saint bring out the real saint in him. His confessions before Velan testify it. He remembers what his mother used to say, 'If there is one good man anywhere, the rains would descend for his sake and benefit the whole world' (pp. 110-111). His real self comes to his rescue and he is driven to think :

> 'If by avoiding food I shall help the trees bloom, and the grass grow why not do it thoroughly?' (pp. 237-38).

At this juncture the supra-individual force, has a certain design for Raju's life. Billy makes such a decision himself when he takes a leap so that the self may be retrieved from decay. Billy is aware of the cosmic force working on him. The divine force acts for Raju for he himself is virtually at the cross-roads of life. He has outlived the hungers of his body and mind, he is now unconcerned with the material world as such. The villagers' faith in the mendicant Raju, brings out the utter meaningless of the worldly prosperity which he had achieved in the course of his earlier life. Both of them dedicate themselves to impersonal causes bigger than themselves. Both Billy and Raju, while being guided to their real selves, come down to the barest elemental simplicity of life. Just as Raju fasts to please the rain God for villagers, Billy stays among tribals for their faith, their love which helps him to understand his self. Both of them have mind boggling, superhuman healing powers which reveal their being in harmony with the elements. Raju is not aware of it yet the 'divine' force relieves him from the sphere of degradation and he develops a new strength to love. Like Billy, Raju also undergoes some painful experiences in the process of his spiritual reawakening. Billy at one point stands midway in his life and takes the path that leads him to his salvation first in love and then in death. When Raju gives up his egocentricity, possesses faith, he is successful in his mission. With his intuition and perception he is able to see beyond the horizon. In the last phase in both the cases, a large number of conscious entities are acting together absolutely with one will and purpose when Billy enters Bilasia's world. He does not feel sad over the working of death and accepts death without hesitation and surprise. For him, death is a precondition of life. The two stories thus reveal triumph of self. The non-melodramaticised deaths of the two protagonists show the effortless merging of their beings into the one common front wherefrom they had emanated. Their quests reveal that the mind-body complex is not the self, but the cosmic spark within the mind-body complex is the self — then the mental turmoil ceases and the mind is fixed on Divine whose expression his body happens to be. At last they are in a thought free state which denotes awareness of reality.

REFERENCES

Arun Joshi, *The Foreigner* (New Delhi : Orient Paperbacks, 1972).

Arun Joshi, *The Strange Case of Billy Biswas* (Bombay : Asia, 1971).

R.K. Narayan, *The Guide* (Mysore : Indian Thought Publications, 1978). All subsequent references are to these cited editions of the novels.

6

A Study of the Corruping Influence of the Technology : *The Strange Case Of Billy Biswas*

SHIVANI VATSA AND RASHMI GAUR

Under the impact of an unprecedented technological avalanche, dark forces of animosity, mutual distrust violence and apathy assail humanity with unchecked vigour. Materialistic aggrandisement and self-delusion have become the guiding factors of human development in all its dimension. The modern man devoid of faith and enlightenment remains in a self-centred vaccum unable to breathe the refreshing air of a liberating truth. Arun Joshi's novels being an incessant search for reality in the present day world, deal with the problems faced by the modern man. In all the novels Joshi has explored the essence of human living and the "mysterious underworld which is the human-soul."[1] His heroes suffer from spiritual uprootedness, cynicism, evils of materialism, loss of faith and crisis of identity under the dual forces of native ethos and Western training.

Arun Joshi carries his study of human predicament in the pretentious, ostentatious and morally and spiritually barren modern world, a step further in the *The Strange Case Of Billy Biswas*. The novel is an attack on the corruption of "civilized" modern life. It brings into our notice the age old Indian culture and civilization. The industrial and technological advancement has created predicament in the society and in the individual. Man cannot realize happiness through mere possession. Eternal joy and happiness can be achieved only through self-realization and spiritual-enlightenment. But, unfortunately, influenced by Western-culture and technological progress, man has forgotten his culture and attaches himself to the mundane fancies and fleeting pleasures of materialistic world. The world today is in a perilious condition because it brushes aside the central questions of the values of life of philosophy and religion as "empty notions and mere fancies."[2]

The rapid scientific and technological progress that man is supposed to be making for himself by his very own hands and mind slowly appears to be turning into a trap. The very comfort, the modern facilities, seems to be oppressing man and the movement of this avalanche has intensified his fears and scepticism and material comfort is comfort no more. The present civilization, may be termed as a scientific civilization : the central weakness of our civilization being the defeat of man by the material.

The Strange Case of Billy Biswas is a continuation of and a development upon the first novel *i.e., The Foreigner*. It continues Sindi's search for identity and meaning of life in this phoney and superficial world but it carries his exploration much deeper than Sindi's. This novel is a severe indictment of the meaningless existence, mechanization, urbanization, discontent, changing values and spiritual uprootedness of the society in the modern civilization. The novel does not merely record the protest of the protagonist, Billy Biswas, against the superficialities of a grossly materialistic civilization and longing for life in a primitive society. It is a study of the total estrangement of its protagonist from the "upper-upper crust of Indian society"[3] with its yearning for materialism, spiritual hollowness and blind imitation of western culture in utter defiance of its traditional values and beliefs.

Billy "man of .....extraordinary obsessions"[4] hailing from the upper crust of society chose to live Harlem the black ghetto in white America because it was "the most human place he could find.... White America was too much civilized for him"[5]. It is here that we have the first glimpse of Billy's dislike for everything phoney, materialistic and superfluous, a trait which later develops to the extent that if forces him to renounce the materialistically advanced society forever.

Billy has an impressive though strange personality . What strikes one about Billy is not only his aristocratic background but also his elegant demeanour : "He was one of those rare men who have poise without pose" One would never fail to notice "the strong, rather British accent of his speech" with "words (that) had a cadence, a compulsive quality that engaged you in spite of yourself". He talked in "soft cultivated voice" "without gestures".[6] He had dark, deep and almost "inhumanly sharp eyes"[7] "which were the dominating feature of his face"[8]. Having an extraordinary power to see "most people who met him considered him a light-hearted good sport without quite noticing the incongruity of his eyes or suspecting what went on in their dark depths."[9] Romi, at a later stage, confesses that "there were many things that I could not see which Billy saw and which step by step led him to the only end that await those who see too much"[10]. For many a times, his face would acquire a peculiar expression and his eyes would narrow "as though trying to unravel some elusive secret of the universe "[11].

Tuula Lindgren ,Billy's Swedish girlfriend and Romi ,the narrator are the only two person "who had any clue to what went on it the dark, inscrutable, unsmiling eyes of Bismal Biswas"[12]. Billy has an extreme fascination for Antropology :

"All I wanted to do in life is to visit the places they describe, meet the people who live there ,find out about the aboriginalness of the world".[13]

Romi was "impressed by the staggering range of his knowledge. What impressed me even more was his passionate involvement with his subject, a thing that was by no means common among the rest of us".[14] He yearns to travel widely in India because India is the home of several primitive "fascinating societies". It gradually dawns on Romi that "it was around his interest in the primitive man that his entire life has been organised"[15].

Billy was aware of a reality other than the tangible one and he had occasional glimpses of the "other side" of life while working with Tuula in mental hospital. Billy has his "first glimpse of the other side"[16]. Billy, there was interested by the simple fact that "people .... Looked at life from a total different point of view."[17] Billy's perception of other world is further intensified by an incident narrated by his father to him. This incident was that a twelve year old boy was sacrificed to propitiate the Goddess Kali so that the young son of a clerk, who was suffering from leukemia could get well. Incidentally, the clerk's son does recover fully, almost within a month of the sacrifice. Billy, however, believes that the son recovered because of the sacrifice as similar cases were reported from the tribal societies of Africa, Indonesia, Japan and from even a country like Sweden. The amazing argument that Billy gives in defence of the act is that it is possible for an ordinary person, having received a message from a goddess in his dream, to sneak into another world for any length of time and then to return to his normal state at the end. He means to say that the clerk, at the time of the crime was operating under the laws of the world other than this world, when his father doesn't believe his, Billy says in great earnestness, "It is only after it happens to oneself that one comes to believe ....All I am saying is that there are worlds at the perphery of this one, above it and below it, and around it , of which we know nothing until we are in them."[18] The intermittent feeling of reality that Billy suffers from and his interest in the primitive people who live outside the vicious circle of modern civilization are given central importance in the first half of the novel. Tuula is perhaps the first person to read Billy's mind correctly. She has "extraordinary intuition" and understands the dilemma of Billy life. Tuula informs Romi that Billy is "an exceptional person" and "feels something inside him... a great force, urkraft, a primitive force. He is afraid of it and tries to suppress it ..... but it is very strong in him, much stronger than in you or me. It can explode any time".[19] It is this primitive force that constantly draws him to primitive world and is responsible to some extent for shaping his unique personality.

Technological progress exercise a significant influence on the pattern of human thinking and understanding. There is a growing tendency for a scientific temper and rational attitude in the individual, but Billy was unlike other individual he had a keen perception, believed in the age old values of life and was untouched by the malicious hands of technology. Billy unfit in the modern civilized world was aware of the persistent hail from the primitive world .Billy hears his first call from primitive world when he is only fourteen year old :

"Yet almost from the very first day almost from the moment that we emerged from the railway station something odds started to work within me."[20]

He felt that a "slumbering part of me has suddenly come awake."[21] However, at this time he was not able to understand the source and the precise nature of this call. He says,

"I could not figure out what excited or troubled me unless it was a sudden interest in my own identity. Who was I? Where has I come from? Where was I going?"[22]

In America too, at the age of twenty he had visions "of being in place other than where I was in place very, very old times a wilderness at other time full of strange primitive people"[23]. Romi, too, observes the primodial urge in Billy at the drum playing session his drumming though not very perfect has "a mesmeric pull" that hold the audience "by it sheer vitality", little package of sound detonated in the smoke filled air in quick succession falling in one rhythm or another creating patterns of sound that deep down, I knew, were not merely that but carried a more fundamental message although what it was, I or Billy for that matter could not have said".[24] When all of a sudden Billy stopped, he was sweating profusely and looked very tired as though "he had returned from a long and difficult journey".[25] Billy frequently discusses with Tuula about his hallucinations who tells him "in very mild form such hallucinations occurred in everyone — all art in a way flowed out of them"[26] but she advises him that "I should not encourage them too much".[27] Out of these hallucinations he come out" very depressed and really shaken up."[28] He described his condition thus :

"I was so shaken up that the first thing I wanted to do was to get back home".[29]

He finds himself "itching to be back"[30], to a congenial atmosphere. His itch for India is an itch for accomplishment of the relevance of life.

Back in India, Billy remains very upset by his hallucinations, he says "I had grown terribly afraid of myself some part of me. I thought terrible things might happen unless I did not do some things drastic. What with being an Indian and having been brought up in a close knit family, the only thing I could think of was to get married. It was like taking out insurance on my normalcy".[31] Meena, his wife represents the hollowness and superficiality of the modern phoney society. Meena fails to satisfy his inner urge. Meena lacks that rare degree of empathy that could have enabled her to understand her husband's vexed mind. Meena's lack of empathy and sufficient idea of human suffering lead to a marital fiasco. "Her upbringing, her ambitions, twenty year of contact with a phoney society — all had ensured that she should not have it. So the more I tried to tell her what was corroding me, bringing me to the edge of despair so to speak, the more resentful she became."[32] And their conjugal-life turned into the "most precarious of battle-fields".[33] Within a year Billy realized that he had committed a blunder. Meena, although is "quite unusually pretty in a westernized sort of way" never short of words and talks "almost entirely in English in that unique, rather flat, accent that is to be found among your ladies taught in convents",[34] she is not able to give peacc and satisfaction that Billy badly require. With the passing of days, Billy starts getting estranged from his family as Meena fails to apprehend his problem. She herself acknowledges to Romi : "Perhaps I just don't understand him as a wife should".[35] Billy's inner restlessness and sense of isolation is enhanced by his failure to establish meaningful contact with his wife and with the society she represents. His "inhumanly sharp eyes" wore a tortured and haggard expression and betrayed "emotions that one tends to associat with a great predicament"[36]. He turns introvert and lackadaisical. Gone was the staggering intelligence, the spectroscopic interests the sense of homour .... the Billy Biswas I had known was finished, snuffed out like a candel left in the rain".[37] Billy does not find meaning or relevance of life either in America or in the civilized Indian society.

The artificial and corrupt society with its phoniness and shallowness seems to smoother Billy's sensibilities and claw him apart. He feels himself "pinned down there like a butterfly"[38]. He feels irritated and disgusted in the civilized modern society. He begins to loss his grips on life and experience a blurring of reality. Thus, though Billy disappears after sometime he cease to belong to the civilized world. The seduction of Rima Kaul an innocent girl in Bombay by Billy is the evidence of his estrangement not only from his family and society but also from his true self. In Arun Joshi's novels the awareness of self is inspired by a confrontation with some crisis.

In case of Billy the seduction of Rima intensifies his urge for self realization .The brief but shameful affair with Rima offers him the first glimpse of his degradation. Though Billy is aware of his "degeneration" yet he fails "to break away from this filth "and turns into a hypocrite and thoroughly corrupt being. He tells Romi,

"It gradually dawned on me that a tremendous corrupting force was working on me. It was though my soul were taking revenge on me for having denied it for so long that other things that it had been clamouring for. Here, you swine, if you have not the guts to break away from this filth, well, then I am going to wallow in it until makes you sick".[39]

Billy realized that his responsibility towards his soul is more than towards the family :

"It was like a warning signal. It was as though a master mind has arranged the whole things to give me preview of what awaited me if I continued to defy its calls."[40]

Billy, thus, has two clear options : "I could either follow this call, this vision, whatever the cost, or be condemned to total decay".[41] He later tells Romi : "Deep down we are afraid that the price of making such choices is terrible not realizing that the prices of not making them is even more terrible".[42]

Billy out of tune with the civilized world is constantly tormented by the persistent call of voice from the uncorrupted world with no pretensions and sophistications. His endeavour to search for a meaningful life and to find his true identity is constantly blurred by his contact with the debasing materialistic and emotionally dehydrated society. The terrible shock that he felt at his own degradation coupled with a "devastating apathy" to his own world and his own family urge him to renounce this sordid meaningless existence in the so- called civilized world. Billy's disappearance into Saal forest of the Maikala hills in Madhya Pradesh is actually the termination of his quest and sojourn in the civilized world. The articulate and strident calls of the primitive world called Billy to join explore and merge with it :

"Come, come to our primitive world that sooner or later overcome the works of man. Come. We have waited for you"[43].

"Come, they cried, it is with us that you begin and with us that you will end .....too longer have you wandered the purlieus of our forbidden city."[44]

"Come, come, come, come..... why do you want to go back? This is all there is on earth .This and the woman waiting for you in the little hut at the bottom of hill. You thought New York was real. You thought New Delhi was your destination. How mistaken you have been, mistaken and misled. Come now, come take us until you have has your fill. It is we who are the inheritors of the cosmic night".[45]

Billy fed up with the greed, avarice, hollowness and hypocrisy of the civilized world eventually broke off all his contacts with the so-called civilized world :

"layers upon layers was peeled off me until nothing but my primitive self was left trembling in the moonlight"[46]

Thus, Billy is now divested of all civilized trappings. Billy's renunciation represents his reaction to the so-called sophisticated way of life. Billy in the civilized world live in a period of agonizing strain, of grave anxiety, of manifold disillusionments. His escape terminated the period of the torment of his soul. Billy is hopeful of leading a meaningful life in the uncorrupted and unsophisticated world.

The excerpts from the letters written by Billy to Tuula confirm that his decision to escape from the civilized world was not taken on a sudden impulse. The first excerpt speaks of his feeling of strangeness in the sophisticated world :

"When I return from an expedition, it is days before I can shake off the sounds and smells of the forest. The curious feeling trails me everywhere that, I am a visitor from the wilderness to the marts of the big city and not the other way round".[47]

Billy's disappearance is not an escape from the realities of life but an escape from the sordid, inept, meaningless existence in the civilized materialistic world into the real life. Billy's escape is a journey from darkness to light, from restlessness to equanimity.

The primitive world held forth immense promise of a life that would nourish Billy and would soothe his otherwise restless and frustrated soul. This novel of Arun Joshi reminds us of D.H. Lawrence's *The Woman Who rode away*. The novelist initially establishes the character of woman (she is always referred to impersonally) and the degradation and utter inanity of the life around her :

"Her surroundings are already so squalidly dead that we can well believe that she would choose another kind of death"[48].

The woman undertook a journey in order to escape from the cataclysm of civilization, to primodial nature. The primodial nature had no connection with the civilized world and was full of rich organic, vital and imperishable life. Billy is terribly sick of the civilized life and the civilized men are estranged to him. Billy develops an intense hatred for them :

"I see a roomful of finely dressed men and women seated on downy sofas .While I am looking at them under my very nose, they turn into a kennel of dogs yawning (their large teeth showing) or snuggling against each other or holding whisky glasses in their furred paws".[49]

The imagery of dogs of large teeth and furred paws show Billy's utter dislike for the elite class and its character. To Billy, the so-called civilized society, to which all the people around belong is "hung on this peg of money and is nothing more than a "heaps of tinsel". He finds civilized societies hollow with preference of money and material progress over personal fulfillment. In one of his letters to Tuula he wonders :

"Whether civilization is anything more than the making and spending of money. What else does the civilized men do?"[50]

These thoughts of Billy remind us of Wordsworth, who in his sonnet 'The World is too much with Us', expresses a deep sense of sorrow at people's sheer money-mindedness and thereby leading to the degradation of their soul :

"The world is too much with us; late and soon,
Getting and spending, we lay waste our powers,
Little we see in nature that is ours;
We have given our hearts away, a sordid boon"[51]

The first part of the novel, reveals the degradation of human values by the material progress of modern civilization. Expressing his disgust over the phoney culture of the Indian upper-class society, Billy tells Romi :

"What got me was the superficialities, the sense of values. I don't think all city societies are as shallow as ours. I am, of course, talking mainly of the so-called upper-classes.........I don't think I have ever met a more pompous, a more mixed up lot of people. Artistically, they were dry as dust. Intellectually, they could no better mechanically mouth ideas that the West abandoned a generation ago. Their idea of romance was to go , and see an American movie or go to one of those wretched restaurants and dance with their wives to a thirty-years old tune. Nobody remembered the old songs or the meaning of the festivals. All the sensuality was gone. So was the poetry. All that was left was loud-mouthed women and men in their three-piece suits dreaming their little adulteries".[52]

Billy is perturbed to find people belonging to the upper classes entirely cut off from their roots especially the younger generation in the blind chase of the Western civilization has neglected the traditional values of its motherhood .Billy is ruffled to see Meena's cousins dancing to a western tune during one of his visits to her house. He recalls : "and the first thing I hear on entering Meena's house is some ten year old American pop record braying like an ass fit to burst, and two of her silly cousins clapping their hands and wiggling their hips as if that was the greatest music of the world. That certainly was not the India I had come back for"[53]. Billy feels that the technological progress of the modern civilization is responsible for the decadence of human values. Billy, tired of meaningless pursuit, in the alien atmosphere of the superficial modern society is haunted by a primitive urge to go into the roots of human existence to find his own identity.

Billy withdraws from the civilized world because the people had started living on a superficial plane with total submission to the materialistic luxuries and comforts. Billy finds this type of living ridiculous and meaningless. While on the other hand, the tribals are innocent and simple-hearted people who know the meaning of suffering and are not hypocrites. They get contentment within their limited resources. He tells Romi :

"What kept us happy, suppose , were the same thing that have kept all primitives happy through the ages : the earth , the forest, the rainbows , the liquor from the mahua, an occasional feast, a lot of dancing and love-making and more then anything else, no ambition, none at all".[54]

Billy himself has no ambition now. The humdrum of the city life on the problems and tensions arising out of making and spending of money no longer disturb the peace and equanimity of his mind. Billy is lured by Bilasia's sensuality,

"Her hair was loose. Just behind her left ear there was a red flower. The necklace of beads glowed a little in the darkness. Her enormous eyes only a little foggier with drink, poured out a sexuality that was nearly as primeval as the forest that surrounded them. Come, come, come, she called and Billy Biswas, son of a Supreme Court Justice went".[55]

Billy's union with Bilasia is not only the union of two bodies but also a union of a split-self to realize the whole. He discovered in her "that bit of himself that he (had) searched for all his life and without which his life (was) nothing more than the poor reflection of a million others."[56] Bilasia was the "strange woman" that had crossed Billy's dream often. Billy once wrote to Tuula :

"A strange woman keeps crossing my dreams. I have seen her on the streets of Delhi, nursing a child in the shade of a tree or hauling stone for a rich man's house. I have seen her buying bangles at a fair. I have seen her shadow at a tribal dance, and I have seen her pensive and inviolable, her clothes clinging to her wet body, besides a tank in Benaras. And once I saw her, her face strangely luminous in the twilight, leading a freight train with sulphur on a siding in one of our eastern parts. Yes, this woman keeps crossing my dreams causing in me a fearful disturbance, the full meaning of which I have yet to understand".[57]

Bilasia is the essence of the primitive force and thus she is able to enliven the soul of Billy, unlike Meena and Rima who had repelled and deadened it .Billy is now no longer interested in thing which provided the sustenance to life in a civilized society.

Dhunia, the head of the tribals, is aware of the fact that Kala Pahar "the black rock" and "master of us all" has called Billy to consummate his search for identity. This search cannot be completed in the imperfect, futile and phoney world of the civilized people but can be accomplished in the shelter of the Kala Pahar. Billy Biswas sick of the modern civilization, abandons it. Billy is entirely transformed. He wears loin-clothes, has grown beard, and is regarded as demi-god by the local tribals, completely tribalised, giving the impression of great vitality. His skin had darkened because of constant exposure to sun. It was stretched tightly emphasizing the muscles of his body. His hair was lighter and longer".[58]

Billy is obstinate in his pursuit of enduring values, for material prosperity fails to deflect him from his search. Billy has no interest in the false, shallow and sordid modern civilization. He is involved in the exploration of his inner-being. Romi rightly remarks :

"If life's meaning lies not in the glossy surfaces of our pretensions but in those dark mossy labyrinths of the soul that languish forever, hidden from the dazzling light of the sun, then I do not know of any man who sought it more recklessly to its call. In brief, I know of no other man who so desperately pursued the tenuous thread of existence of its bitter end, no matter what trails of glory or shattered hearts he left behind in his turbulent wake".[59]

Billy's awareness of the deeper layers of his personality makes him an estranged and alienated person in the contemporary society which identifies only the superficial realities of life. He attempts to find out viable alternatives for the modern man tapped in the vicious circle of materialism. Romi, the narrator conveys the same in the opening of the novel :

"As I grow old, I realize that the most futile cry of man is his impossible wish to be understood. The attempt to understand is probably even more futile. If in spite of this I propose to relate Billy's story, it is not so much because I claim to have understood his as it is on account of a deep and unrelieved sense of wonder that in the middle of the twentieth century, in the heart of Delhi's smart society, there should have lived a man of such extraordinary obsessions".[60]

Arun Joshi makes us aware of an alternative mode of living which is a total contrast to the materialistic society, devoid of any sense of purpose, direction and values. Billy was contented in his primitive life and all his restlessness was replaced by a serenity.

Billy with his healing touch and knowledge of the herbal medicines cured Situ, Romi's wife, of an agonizing chronic migraine. This incident gives the story a turn. Billy had warned Romi not to disclose about his whereabouts to anybody. He cautions Romi : "If they ever get hold of me, they will not leave me alone. And you know what havoc it will play with my life here".[61] However things go beyond Romi's control and his pestering wife compels him to disclose the secret and lets Meena and Mr. Biswas know about Billy's being alive. Romi tries his best to protect Billy from the destructive hands of the civilized world. But Billy's father, a one time ambassador and retired supreme court judge sets the whole government machinery moving to trace Billy with an idea" to drag him upto Delhi by force".[62] A young and enthusiastic IPS officer, Mr. Rele, is appointed to execute this plan. Rele belongs to a society which, with its middle-class mentality does not hesitate in branding men like Billy as "irresponsible fools" and "common criminals"[63] and can go to any limit in preventing them from going astray from the norms. His approach is purely mechanical devoid of any sensitivity or understanding of human psyche and is juxtaposed with Billy. The more Romi tried to convince them of the undesirability of their efforts, the more "they converted the story...... into a stereotype childish escapade which was all that their ordinary minds were capable of"[64]. Consequently "the search of Billy is turned .... into a man-hunt".[65] Despite Romi's best efforts of avoid the tragedy, Billy is shot dead by a havildar.

> " 'Billy', I cried. 'Billy'.
>
> He opened his fast-glazing eyes for a moment and appeared to look at me.
>
> 'You bastard's he said hoarsely. Then he died"[66].

In the last two words uttered by Billy, "You bastards", he slaps his verdict on this inhumane world which knows no other way of' disposing its rebels, its seers, its true lovers"[67]. Romi is deeply grieved by the unbearably tragic end of Billy and reflects :

> "gradually it dawned upon us that what we had killed was not a man , not even the son of a "Governor",

> but some one for whom our civilized world had no equivalent. It was as though, we had killed one of the numerous man — god of the primitive pantheon"[68].

Billy, who had dared "to step out its stifling confines"[69] ultimately had to pay price with his life for not conforming to the norms of the so-called civilized society. The civilized world eventually destroyed him. Billy's case is terribly pathetic and it criticizes the insufferable suffocation caused by the present modern materialistic society.

Billy a "refugee from civilization"[70] feels established in the primitive world where he finds his identity, his roots. When the people from the civilized world try to take him back, he prefers to die rather than succumbing to their black and deep desires. Billy's end was "as certain as the end of solitary boats beating against the maelstrom"[71]. Arun Joshi, in this novel, reiterates the tyranny of the forces of the phoney civilization that crushes man's desires for self-realization and kinship with nature. The character of Billy represents the dehumanizing impact of modern life on the individuals. The turmoil experienced in the materialistic world is resolved by the mental and spiritual tranquility, solace and contentment of the primitive life. When Romi asks Billy : "But, don't you think you had responsibilities towards her, towards your son?" He replies : "I had greater responsibilities towards my soul"[72]. Thus, Billy escapes from the corrupting influence of the civilized society to lead a meaningful life in the peaceful sanctuary of the primitive world.

Arun Joshi while dealing with the meaningless existence of man in this modern world, has also tried to present solutions to the problems. In *The Strange Case of Billy Biswas*, through the characterization of Billy, Joshi suggests a different approach. As Billy proved, if one is able to establish compatibility with the primitive life, one can get rid of all the problems of life. Arun Joshi, in this novel, unravels the facets of identity crisis in modern man's life living in the world by opportunism, treachery, cowardice, hypocrisy and wit. The novel is a powerful indictment of the modern civilization depicting Billy's fulfillment of his longing to locate his real-self in the primitive civilization and not in the matrix of the westernized culture. Billy, in many ways, remind us of Querry, the protagonist of Graham Greene's *A Burnt Out Case*.

A successful and renowned architect of Europe, Querry, relinquished the materialistic life and went to the remote Congo region in the Central Africa to live with the socially — ousted lepers in quest of inner peace and self-knowledge . Like Billy, his search too remains unfulfilled due to his untimely death caused by the intervening of the modern world. Samuell Beckett's novel *Murphy*, too, deals with similar theme. The hero of the novel, Murphy, absconds from the civilized world. The basic human emotions which had perished in the materialistic way of life are resuscitated when he lived and served in an asylum for lunatics as a male nurse. Murphy, in the same manner as Billy is hunted by the representatives of the civilized world and dies midway. Of all the protagonists, Billy alone is able to overcome the predicament of modern man successfully and convincingly. He is thus presented in the form of a rebel while others are depicted as helpless compromisers. Billy, in order to engage himself for the exploration of the essence of human living renounced the outer world of physical attractions and temptations. His renunciation is reminiscent of Siddhartha's renunciation of wife and child along with the luxuries of the materialistic world in search of the ultimate truth about human existence. The pernicious impact of rapid industrialization and urbanization digresses man from the very purpose of his life.

Due to Billy's untimely death, his quest for something higher and nobler, something nobler remains incomplete in the same manner as that of the sculptor king who failed to carve the face of god. The novelist, in this novel, has dealt with the chaotic state of man in the modern world, the world which is engulfed within the detrimental and abominable claws of technology. The contradictions and the aimlessness in Billy's character is due to the nostalgic predilection for the native culture to which he is exposed. The soul-destroying, meaningless, mechanical, monotonous, moronic existence is an insult to human nature.

Arun Joshi suggests that the technology development has taken a wrong turn and needs to be redirected. The technology is felt to be becoming more and more inhumane. The man dominated by technology does not posses the virtues of being self-balancing, self-adjusting and self-cleansing. It is quite sure that the way of life which bases on materialism cannot last long because the human nature revolts against the inhumane technological advancement which it experiences as suffocating and debilitating. The technology must be redirected so that it serves man instead of destroying him. Modern man has lost the meaningful of life and is smothering in the decadent civilized world.

However, Joshi says that the modern civilization can be saved by love of truth and beauty, sympathy with the oppressed and beliefs in the brotherhood of man, justice and mercy, and above all by limitation of the machinery." The machines should not be allowed to cripple the limbs of man."[73] By following our age-old spiritual culture, Joshi believes that the scientific civilization can be made to save humanity from suffering and destruction. Thus, the task before man is to marshal more of technology to the service of human purposes, not to put technology in to a self-destruct sand reverse- thyself gear. Thus, as Gandhi once said : "I am aiming not a eradication of all machinery, but limitation."[74] Technological and scientific progress is beneficial for man but only when it remains within a proper limit and doesn't transgress it. Thus, Billy provides solution to the human predicament in the contemporary society by suggesting to pursue an alternative, simple and meaningful existence.

REFERENCES

1. An interview with Sujata Mathai, "I am a stranger to my books" (*Times of India*, July 7, 1983). p. 8.
2. S. Radhakrishnan, *Religion and Society*, (London, George Allen and Unwin Ltd. 1969) p. 9.
3. Arun Joshi, *The Strange Case of Billy Biswas* (New Delhi, Hind Pochet Books, 1971) p. 9.
4. *Ibid.*, p. 7.
5. *Ibid.*, p. 9.
6. *Ibid.*, p. 11.
7. *Ibid.*, p. 43.
8. *Ibid.*, p. 12.
9. *Ibid.*
10. *Ibid.*, p. 40.
11. *Ibid.*, p. 35.
12. *Ibid.*, p. 19.
13. *Ibid.*, p. 14.

14. *Ibid.*
15. *Ibid.*
16. *Ibid.*, p. 18.
17. *Ibid.*, p. 19.
18. *Ibid.*, pp. 54-55.
19. *Ibid.*, p. 23.
20. *Ibid.*, p. 122.
21. *Ibid.*
22. *Ibid.*
23. *Ibid.*, p. 180.
24. *Ibid.*, p. 21.
25. *Ibid.*
26. *Ibid.*, p. 181.
27. *Ibid.*
28. *Ibid.*
29. *Ibid.*
30. *Ibid.*, p. 27.
31. *Ibid.*, p. 182.
32. *Ibid.*, p. 185.
33. *Ibid.*, p. 81.
34. *Ibid.*, p. 37.
35. *Ibid.*, p. 76.
36. *Ibid.*, p. 44.
37. *Ibid.*, p. 70.
38. *Ibid.*, p. 47.
39. *Ibid.*, p. 189.
40. *Ibid.*
41. *Ibid.*, p. 190.
42. *Ibid.*
43. *Ibid.*, p. 120-21.
44. *Ibid.*, p. 141.
45. *Ibid.*, p. 121.
46. *Ibid.*
47. *Ibid.*, p. 96.
48. Graham Hough, *The Dark Sun : A Study of D.H. Lawrence* (London : Gerald Duckworth, 1966) p. 141.
49. Arun Joshi, *op. cit.*, p. 96.

50. *Ibid.*, p. 97.

51. William Wordsworth, *Wordsworth Poetry and Prose*, (London, Rupert Hart-Davis, 1955) p. 536.

52. Arun Joshi, *op. cit*, p. 179.

53. *Ibid.*, p. 60.

54. *Ibid.*, p. 148.

55. *Ibid.*, pp. 141-42.

56. *Ibid.*, p. 142.

57. *Ibid.*, p. 97.

58. *Ibid.*, p. 102.

59. *Ibid.*, p. 8.

60. *Ibid.*, p. 7.

61. *Ibid.*, p. 151.

62. *Ibid.*, p. 207.

63. *Ibid.*, p. 231.

64. *Ibid.*, p. 206.

65. *Ibid.*, p. 232.

66. *Ibid.*, p. 233.

67. *Ibid.*, p. 240.

68. *Ibid.*, p. 236.

69. *Ibid.*, p. 240.

70. *Ibid.*, p. 140.

71. *Ibid.*, p. 240.

72. *Ibid.*, p. 186.

73. Shiva Nand Jha, "A Critical Study of Gandhian Economic Thought" (Agra, Laxminarayan Aggarwal, 1955) p. 126.

74. *Ibid.*, p. 128.

7

Indian Ethos in Arun Joshi's *The Last Labyrinth*

M. MANI MEITEI

Indian English literature originated as a necessary outcome of the introduction of English education in India under the colonial rule. The new literature, however, is characterized by Indian themes, Indian reality and, above all, by a new language, that is, a new English, adequately suitable for the communication of Indian experience.

Indian English literature is today a fast-growing discipline at the levels of creativity and criticism. The earlier shackles, skepticism and cynicism with which the new literature was born, have vanished with the passage of time. Today this literature, which was born on Indian soil in the hands of Indians, is widely acclaimed even outside the land of its birth. Speaking about Indian English fiction, Braj B. Kachru remarks :

> Indian English fiction is now being studied and discussed in the entire English-speaking world by those interested in the Indian subcontinent or in non-native Englishes, and by linguists for its thematic and stylistic Indianness. At least half a dozen Indian English novelists have created a small but slowly increasing international reading public for themselves, *e.g.*, Mulk Raj Anand, Anita Desai, Manohar Malgonkar, Kamala Markandaya, R.K. Narayan, Raja Rao, Khushwant Singh and Nayantara Sahgal.[1]

Obviously, international attention to these Indian writers is due to their Indianness conveyed through their work in more ways than one, including themes, images, myths, symbols and linguistic nuances. Typical Indian themes are said to be : "the caste system, social attitudes, social and religious taboos, superstitions, notions of superiority and inferiority."[2] Even more important issues pertain to socio-cultural ethos and philosophical heritage. Moreover, as K.S. Srinivasan aptly points out. myths are also repositories of Indian identity :

> .... The characteristic Indianness is traceable to the totality of the myth of India embodied in themes such as Siva-Parvati, Radha-Krishna, Rama-Sita and so on, they being part of our collective national psyche.... Tales from *Panchatantra, Kathasamsatgara,* and the extinct *Brihatkatha* are as much part of the national psyche.[3]

It would be interesting to see how these dominant themes and myths are used in Indian English novels. With the gradual breakdown of the monopoly of English literature, now better known as British literature, the centrality has shifted and literature written in new Englishes has begun to demand equal recognition. As Alastair Niven remarks,

> Commonwealth Literature is all about the shift away from the notion of centrality. Far from attempting to impose unity upon diversity, to force a Eurocentric precision of focus on many different cultures, it recognises a multiplicity of equally valid centres, but then proceeds to evaluate their individual absorption of local influences.

Thus, Indian English literature is today one of the most authentic voices of India. In order to express Indian ethos it has made a distinctive departure from the earlier English literature both in style and in the treatment of themes expressive of national psyche and cultural consciousness. It is not time for one to look at British literature with awe and wonder, rather one has to get inspiration from Indian literature both ancient and modern as Eliot. Yeats, etc. did. One has also to explore and evaluate their interconnections and convergences so that transmission of cultural values gets assimilated. Thus, indeed, will lead to other fields of great interest like comparative studies. But that will be another matter altogether. The present paper is devoted to the discussion of Arun Joshi's *The Last Labyrinth* from the point of view of Indian culture and ethos to see how far Joshi has Indianized English language and literature creatively.

II

Arun Joshi is one of the leading Indian English novelists who have been actively writing in the second half of the present century. Of the four novels he has written till date, *The Strange Case of Billy Biswas* (1971) and *The Last Labyrinth* (1981) are a class by themselves. *The Last Labyrinth* is unparalleled in the treatment of a subtle Indian theme based on the import of Hindu religious philosophy as advocated in the holy scriptures like the *Gita* and the Upanishads. The book is about man confronted by the four paths of life : *dharma* (duty), *artha* (wealth), *kama* (desire) and *moksha* (liberation). It is based on the *karma yoga,* the attainment of liberty by the soul by abandoning *kama* (desire), *krodh* (anger), *lobha* (greed), *moha* (allurement), *mada* (lust) and *aiswarya* (pride), the six enemies of man. The book is so deeply influenced by the Hindu religious scriptures that all that happens in the book is guided by the principles of *Hindu Sastras* and thoughts.

It is the basic principles of Hindu life which provide the necessary framework to *The Last Labyrinth* ranging from the creation of characters to the underlying currents and cross-currents of the whole structure. The novel derives its roots from the Upanishads. It deals with the journey of man from the temporal to the immutable centre. The novelist, while centering round the two conflicting hungers, "Hunger of the body, Hunger of the spirit",[5] suggests the path of human salvation. He adds : "Your body is God's chariot, says Tuka Ram." (10) The idea has been derived from the Upanishads :

> Atmanam rathinam viddhi shariram rathmevahi,
> Indriyam hayam dhuh manah pragrahmeva cha.
>
> (*Kathopanisad* 3/3)

In English translation it reads thus : "Know the soul as chariot rider. The body is the chariot. Ten organs are the horses of the chariot and mind is the bridle." In order to have a balanced personality the mind is to be kept under control, and the control of mind, though difficult, is to be done through two things, *i.e.* practice and renunciation, as Lord Krishna says to Arjuna in the *Gita*. The *karmayoga* presupposes an equilibrium through the equation of *dharma*, *artha* and *kama*. Once this harmony is attained, the path to *moksha* is smooth, and the final renunciation of the body, the chariot of the soul, takes place in full realization of the Ultimate Soul.

In *The Last Labyrinth* the protagonist, Som Bhaskar, is the battleground between the two hungers of body and spirit. And in the fight his mind takes side with the body. Being overpowered by desire, he falls a victim to *kama* and other accompanying vices such as lust, wrath, greed and pride. The successive pages of the novel, especially the first part, unfold his indomitable hunger for sex. His excessive preoccupation with sex makes him a miniature Casanova, for he is, in the words of Leela Sabnis, a "compulsive fornicature" (80). The book, thus, gives a healthy expression to the forces of *Id*. Thick with desire, and the path of *moksha* being illusive, for he himself is blind to it, he goes for passion, responding to the ancient music of desire that either he hears or his unconscious self sings : "I want, I want, I want, I want", that appears and reappears in the novel time and again. And this hunger the fulfils with Anuradha, an antique looking woman, who is like "a monument : tall, handsome, ruined...thirty, thirtyfive...from Bengal, from Sikkim, from the valleys of Nepal" (12) and who possesses the characteristics of medieval courtesans "around whom wars might have been fought" (133). It is in his effort to possess her wildly and madly that she becomes the centre of his life in both bodily and spiritual terms. Gargi rightly conveys this when she writes to Som : "She (Anuradha) is your shakti" (121). For she is a real shakti who can transform Som's hunger of the body into hunger of the spirit. To him making love to Anuradha is a kind of eternal renewal of his search for the last labyrinth, which he believes he will get in sexual communion. Therefore, with his eternal question, "what is in the last labyrinth?", his sexual possession of Anuradha ever increases with ferocity each time they meet. Anuradha, on her part, does evade the question from being solved, perhaps with the conviction that one has to quest for this oneself. Ultimately, the last labyrinth turns out to be the realization of the existence of God or the death of the body and consequent liberation of the soul. In the whole process of this march of human soul from the darkness of *maya* to renunciation the novelist's emphasis is on the practical philosophy of *karmayoga*, which unlike *sanyasa* (abandonment of worldly affairs and actions after self-realization, as Gautama Buddha did), does not aim at "giving up worldly affairs but continuing to perform them in such a way that they do not create any difficulty in the matter of obtaining Release."[6]

The title of the novel, *The Last Labyrinth*, is highly significant. It stands for the great mystery that hangs about the book's deep structure, and is itself a matter of great inquiry. Labyrinth has been defined as "the complex prison built by Daedalus for King Minos of Create to contain the Minotaur. The name probably is derived from *labrys*, the sacred double axe of the Creatans, and there was the temple of bull cult in Crete. So complicated was the Labyrinth that none could escape once it was entered.... The name was applied not only to buildings....but to all kinds of mazes."[7] The labyrinth in the novel is many-faceted. One is Aftab's Lal Haveli, a prison-like earthly labyrinth, where Som enters and is trapped in a maze without his knowing, as if he were under a magic spell. As for the Haveli, "There are things about such houses that you discover only with time" (33). Aftab says the Haveli was built like a labyrinth because "My ancestors baffled their enemies this way. There are rooms within rooms, corridors that only bring you back to where you started" (36-37). He further adds : "There are rooms where you could lock a man up and he would never be found. No one would hear his cry" (37). To Som the maroon Blue Room where he is welcomed by Aftab and Anuradha seems to be the last labyrinth. And his own inability to escape from it proves the prison-like character of the house. The fact that Som is inseparable from the rest of the inmates in the haveli is symbolically revealed when he sees his own image in the midst of portraits in the Blue Room :

> Turning a corner I was startled by an apparition. Careworn, holding a cigarette in one hand, it looked

> as though for many centuries it had lived in that bleak house I stared breathless, realizing, suddenly, that I was staring at my own image. (32)

Anuradha is the force that makes Som a captive in that haveli. Anuradha represents a constellation of stars and Som stands for the moon for a creeper, from which medicinal juice is extracted, and the moon is believed to be the giver of the medicinal juice. Bhaskar is, again, the sun, that gives light, and enlightens others. Their relationship therefore is one of the moon, the stars and the sun. The hidden meaning of the novel can be worked out by studying the novel in terms of these symbols.

Another symbolic meaning of the labyrinth is associated with sex. The attraction of Som and Anuradha leads to their being sexual partners, no matter what they are, for he is married and has two daughters, and she is Aftab's mistress or unmarried wife. The sight of Anuradha and her *mehandi* revives his latent passion or physical hunger kept repressed for years. To him sex is a mystery, and he wants to know what is in the last sexual labyrinth. His lust after sex is symbolized by the peacock with unfurled tail woven into the carpet of the room which is given to him and where he sleeps with Anuradha. Contrary to this, Som's spiritual quest in the last part of the novel signifies a yet another meaning of the last labyrinth. He slowly recognises the existence of God when he does penance, after his wasteful indulgent life. As O.P. Mathur aptly remarks "*The Last Labyrinth* seems to depict the vague but unmistakably reaching out for faith and understanding by a man lost in the labyrinth of desires and the vague simmerings of his discontent with this type of life."[8] All this shows the overall complexity of this highly symbolic novel. Without taking cognizance of the implicit cultural and religious context of the novel its embedded meaning will remain surrounded by obscurity.

The central character of the novel, Som, is a fusion of two conflicting human faculties, instinct and reason. This blend of two distinctly separate sides of human faculty corresponds with the basic thematic background of the novel. Instinct is the very ground of *kama* to which Som responds with a sense of immediacy. His reasoning enables him to seek the evidence of the existence of God Encircled by the world of *maya* and voids, he becomes a "sad man" (56) losing his head unable to guide himself in the direction of the right path, *i.e., dharma.* Leela Sabnis rightly regards him as "A man so successful, so intelligent", and asks, "why should such a man be so confused"? (79). Explaining his voids, their cause and effect, she says, "....may be what you want is a mystical identification, identification with a godhead, as most Hindus want, sooner or later" (113). Gargi, Anuradha and even Geeta know that what he needs is not *kama* but *moksha*. Anuradha oliquely says to him : "It is not me you want." She goes on saying, "I know. You want something. You badly want something. I could see that the first time we met. But it is not me. That, too, I can see. I told you so in the dargah" (58-59). Everybody wants to waken his soul from darkness to light. Here lies the novel's root in *dharma*, that advocates that true faith can take over the difficulties of the mundane affairs and temporal values of life.

The darkness of the lapsed soul is obviously caused by the overweight of the affairs of *kama*. Som and Aftab are least disturbed by other affairs, including money, though they are big industrialists. "I know that", says Som, "money was dirt, a whore. So were houses, cars, carpets" (11). The buying and selling of shares, meetings at Intercontinental Hotel constitute their path of *artha*, a superficial cover of their lives. Inside they are trying to fulfil their carnal desires. While Som remains highly sexed, Aftab, like his ancestors who "lived from day to day and impulse to impulse", lives "Insides the city, dancing and drinking..." (40). It is not a meaningful means of livelihood, but is a means of fulfilling their desires. For Som it is through his business that he comes to Lal Haveli to snatch Anuradha away from Aftab, and then to grab the latter's business in spite of Anuradha's entreaty to leave Aftab alone. Surrounded by hedonistic ideas, Aftab satisfies himself with Azizun, a dancer. Som and Aftab are, thus, described as plunderers of Benaras, as the former reflects : "Benaras is a city set in an oasis, plundered a thousand times and waiting to be plundered again by men like Aftab and me who forever lurked in its desert purlieus" (37). The general drift of affairs is thus towards the world of *kama*. Som takes possession of Anuradha at will; he comes and goes to and from Benaras like the wind, much to the embarrassment of Aftab, who in his heart of hearts suffers the pain of humiliation and is broken into pieces.

Som's irresistable passions go on in violent intoxication till his anti-climactic fall with a massive heart attack, from which his question of survival would and have come at all had not Anuradha and Gargi come to his rescue under miraculous circumstances. Thereafter he loses sight of Anuradha, and even his attempts to talk to her on phone prove to be of no avail. It is the most crucial turning point in the novel's development. Anuradha slips out of Som's hand, and her unseen presence works upon Som's mind. Yet the cannot accept the rush of events as he suspects a foul game unleashed against him by Aftab. Now all his energies of desire and lust are converted into anger, greed and hatred and he hatches plans to cripple Aftab's business in retaliation for his failure to meet Anuradha. He mortgages his plants and lands to purchase the outstanding shares of Aftab's company. He knows the greater and deeper part of him belongs to Anuradha, in whose thought he feels happy with a sort of warm radiation. His very root shelters in the physical body of Anuradha — her breasts, thighs, sari-clad body, her *mehandi*, the tattoo mark on her forehead as a permanent *bindi*, and her scented body. Of Krishna he takes no notice, and his intellect seems to accept Darwin's evolution theory. His religion is to worship body and he takes shelter in *kama*. He says : "...we coupled high above the earth, independent of time and space, like a pair of asteroids, locked in each other's gravity...we communicated through the thrust and push and pull of our bodies...the most intimate dialogues" (107).

A notable feature of Arun Joshi's heroes is that while they are highly placed both by training and by profession in the society, they are not society's men. They are driven by forces unknown and irrational, and all their actions are not intelligible to the rational mind. They are individuals who have very rich life-within rather than life-without and are subject almost by instinct to an unconscious link with the primal world, the original picture of the world. Their inability to eschew this world keeps them awake to the promptings and voices of this world thereby rendering them highly contemptuous of reason. Billy Biswas and Som Bhaskar may look preposterous, but their complexity has other facets of their illusive characters.

Sindi Oberoi and Ratan Rathor are also deeply disturbed characters being confined themselves to their private worlds. Like Billy who is searching for "worlds within worlds."[9] Som is searching for a labyrinth within the labyrinth. Their English education and western degrees are of little help to discard their unconscious bond with age-old Indian ethos and cultural heritage. Arun Joshi very ably deals with this theme of emotional dominance of man over his intellectual and orthodox values of life, stressing the need for the individual to remain faithful to life, responding to it in a healthy primitive manner. His heroes — especially Som and Billy — seek refuge in a mystical primitivism, physically running away from the fact-finding, mechanized, urban, sophisticated life. Som's faith is in the intuitive religion based on the fundamental instincts of man, which vent themselves upon an immediacy of fulfilment of a strong primitive desire. In him alone can one see the two kinds of men as found in Hardy — "the gentleman and the peasant" and also Lawrence's sophisticated, rich, intellectuals and unintellectuals, highly sexed characters full of smouldering, sullen energy. In Som's wild hunt for physical pleasure reason hardly enters, and, again, when he talks of God his intellect seeks the proof of the existence of God. This amounts to his disbelief in God or His existence. He attributes the death of his mother to her wrong faith in Krishna, which prevented others from taking her to a hospital to cure her cancer. Later he comes to know that Anuradha's mother also was a victim of the same false faith in Krishna. When she said that she was married to Krishna, the man in a fit killed her with a broken whisky bottle.

Lack of faith, however, does not do Som any good. He is suffering from tension, unhappiness, disturbance, hysteria, tantrum, neurosis, and some strange dreams and insomnia while all others around him are happy even in suffering and in face of death. His mother was never saddened by the thought of death; rather she enjoyed life thinking that she would be saved and cured by the wooden image of Krishna. Tuka Ram says : "God realizes Himself in the devotion of His worshippers. Likewise, faith is essential to their realization of Him."[10] It is faith that gives peace and happiness. Som's suffering, however, is on account of his fear of death. He admits : "I was insecure....I was afraid of death. That made a little more sense. I was mortally afraid of death" (74). To his questions, "what is the First Cause?" and "what is in the last labyrinth?" he gets the answer as 'death'. When his father died he got the First Cause. To Aftab also what remains in the last labyrinth is "Why, death, of course" (37). He feels diffident, discontent, and knows that "If discontent is my trademark, trust is Geeta's" (63). In a tone of feeble repentance for disbelief he remembers Kierkegaard, who says : "Prayer does not change God but it changes him who prays" (118). Som's is, however, a tortured soul, in which all forces of *maya* are let loose, he hears voices, as he complains : "All my life I have heard voices....I hear them a little too often and a little too loud. Voices, mostly of the dead...rclatives, authors, scoundrels, saints..." (68).

At last the light of *moksha* dawns upon Som as if the whole universe had come out of a void. Now he has to undergo a path of renunciation, which he begins skeptically because of his guilt. Anuradha whom he knows in physical terms, now untraceable, is capable of spiritual union with the Lord, and is beyond reach : "She was like the ocean; one could never reach the bottom of her" (132). Knowing that he is a man with a sick soul, she asks him to look at a god up the mountains where lepers are waiting for the mercy of the Lord to cure their disease. This is the first light of *dharma* that opens his eyes. For getting salvation the first and foremost task is not only renunciation of desires of all kinds but self-realization. Som for the first time looks within and sees that he is a leper : "Deep inside my heart I knew I was a leper, that I needed a cure" (126). His faith in God or Lord Krishna is, thus, derived from Anuradha, who is a messenger or *bhakta* of the Lord. Earlier Leela Sabnis, who knew that Som was a neurotic and whose problems could not be solved by a psychiatrist, prescribed Descartes to cure his disease. The reference to Descartes is to inculcate the idea that the existence of God is the very genesis of all in the universe and that the refusal to believe in Him would lead modern man to a sense of rootlessness and alienation. Descartes also advocates self-control as the first step to the attainment of spiritual freedom. Frederick Mayer says :

> Descartes tried to know that by controlling our desires with inner fortitude and by making ourselves

> independent of the world, we can live a really philosophical life. We must not be diverted from our goal by sensuous longings. The great ideal which he had before him was spiritual freedom. He considered the intellectual love for God to be ultimately the greatest moral virtue.[11]

Som's development from the darkness of body to the awareness of spirit might have been possible through Descartes philosophy. But Indian philosophy, which is rooted to its great tradition of the Vedas, the Upanishads and the *Gita*, seems to have completed the process of Som's slow realization and the end of a long drama of abasement in *kama*. The long rope of his life is now tightened so that he does not go astray and listens to the Lord. His anguish for physical pleasure gets slowly dissolved in timelessness. One can reckon with what the *Gita* says : "Sensual pleasures are the source of pain/For they have a beginning and an end/So the illuminate cannot rejoice in them."[12]

The last labyrinth cannot be achieved through the path of *kama*. On the Janmasthami day Anuradha takes Som to witness the birth of the Lord and pay his respects to Him. "She had wanted me to visit the God, walk up a steep mountain road and pay my respects" (130). His coming to the holy city of Benaras is not only to plunder its treasure but also to purify his sick and weary soul, for getting the higher harmony. But that does not come in an easy way : one has to conquer desire, temptations, anger, lust, greed and pride. Som is greatly disturbed by them even when he goes to the shrine, he is agitated by the memory of Anuradha, his "lips against her throat" and the thought makes him fall "into a bottomless pit of despair, like a shipwrecked sailor sinking into the ocean" (147). Being ignorant of the last goal of life, *moksha*, he continues to suffer, gripped by a vague fear of everything. He is hardly different from people mentioned in the *Gita* by Lord Krishna : "...these ignorant men/Not knowing me, in my essence, stumble and fall".[13]

Finally the words of Anuradha that "There is a god in those mountains" (157) stir Som profoundly. He wants to go to the mountains to do penance. In his search for the Lord he undertakes an unending pilgrimage with concomitant inner tension. Still one of the haunting questions is whether God exists or not. He goes to the shrine where there is a deity beside which a flame burns and kneels in front of it, but gets excited at the thought of Anuradha. Much troubled, he goes to Gargi with the question regarding the existence of God. He is also beset by anger and greed, for he fails to meet Anuradha. Hearing him react so, "Gargi laughed, then wrote on her pad, 'God does not work in this simple manner, God does not seek revenge...'" (213). True God or His existence is to be meditated upon and not to be argued with logic and analysis. Men should waste no time in argument", says Tuka Ram, "but throw themselves at God's feet." Science only begins and ends with evidence. To disdain logic and science Anuradha says : "May be Krishna begins where Darwin left off" (132). And to get *moksha* one must make a complete surrender or submission to the will of God. To question His existence is completely ruled out in theology. The one who worships Him can get Him. Lord Krishna says : "The ones who worship the gods go to the gods/But my dear devotees come to me" (*Gita* 7 : 23).

The much sought-after last labyrinth is the last stage of man's spiritual journey, the stage of self-liberation. This reminds one of the artifice of eternity in Yeats's Byzantium poems both in the thematic and symbolic development. The Indian concept of *moksha* is a result of long meditation, suppression of desires, lust, anger, greed etc. Gargi observes : "We are all children trying to reach up to a crack in the door to peep into a room" (24). Perhaps, now it is Som's turn to realize : "One had probably to rise up to the crack by oneself" (215). Som ultimately comes to a meaningful stage of his pilgrimage. He begins to regard Anuradha as a sign of his final awareness.

> Anuradha, listen, listen to me wherever you are. Is there a God where you are? Have you met Him? Does He have a face? Does He speak? Does He hear? Does He understand the language that we speak? Anuradha, if there is a God and if you have met Him, and if He is willing to listen, then, Anuradha, my soul, tell Him, tell this God to have mercy upon me. Tell Him I am weary. Of so many fears, so much doubting. Of this dark earth and these empty heavens.

> Plead for me, Anuradha. He will listen to you (222-23).

This re-echoes Arjuna's final submission to Lord Krishna to guide him and show the light of the true path of life :

> Afflicted with the weakness of self-pity,
> With my mind in a turmoil, I see no way out.
> So in this blind gloom flash the lead of light
> To me, thy disciple I seek refuge in thee.
>
> (*Gita* 2 : 7)

The Last Labyrinth as a work of art has a great moral purpose, *i.e.*, edification of human soul by following the path of *dharma*. Only *dharma* can guide a man through the meandering paths of life. The emphasis falls on a harmonious balance of three paths of life — *karma, jnana* and *bhakti*. The novel is as much about man's action, knowledge and devotion as it is about the liberation of human soul, attained by living in a sin-tainted world of *kama, krodha, lobha, moha, mada* and *aiswarya* but free from the perilous influences of them all. The novelist has vindicated the importance of *bhakti* (*i.e.*, humility, kindness, truthfulness, contentment and peaceableness) and knowledge of Release and God without abandoning action.

Arun Joshi's greatness as a novelist in *The Last Labyrinth* is that in this novel he does not try to present his vision of life from the Western point of view. In a refreshingly new way he moulds his art out of Hindu religious philosophy and the preachings of saints and divines, all of whom speak of the harmonious development of man's physical, mental and spiritual powers as the highest form of all creations. Arun Joshi, an original and successful artist as he is, has thus enriched through creative potential of English through the great Indian tradition.

III

When an artist chooses a language as the medium of expression, he has to be amply sure that it serves as an effective means to convey what he intends to communicate. It would be worthwhile to see how Joshi uses English to represent Indian ethos and experience. Raja Rao once said : "One has to convey in a language that is not one's own the spirit that is one's own." This sums up the problems that a writer writing in an adopted language has to face. The Nigerian novelist Chinua Achebe was not unaware of the change. He said : "I feel that the English language will be able to carry the weight of my African experience. But it will have to be a new English, still in full communion with its ancestral home altered to suit its new African surroundings."[14] Similarly, Joshi has transmitted his Indian experience in a language startlingly his. The idiom that he employs for the treatment of Indian themes and experience is both innovative and experimental and manifests the strength and newness of the twice-born English language in India.

Joshi has made sincere efforts to authenticate his thematic projection by Indianization of English language. His choice of words from the Indian sources gives him a new mode of expression to go with his Indian experience. *The Last Labyrinth* uses Indian words like *mehandi, dargah, motia, bindi, sarangii, raat-ki-raani, Lal Haveli, nullah, purdah, palki, hukka, chup-chup, churidars, salaam, kurta, kathak, ghunghrus, tablas, namaskar,* etc. How some of these words fit in the narrative and evoke the desired atmosphere may be seen in the passage given below :

> Still later, the girl was dancing, a mere child, thin and wispy in her costume of a *kathak* dancer. Her little feet, so like a pair of pink birds, played with the smooth floor. The *ghunghrus* mingled with the wail of the *sarangii* [originally not italicized], kept beat with the *tablas*. Her eyes, the neck, the full mouth and the little hands, gesticulated, suggested, built up, gesture by gesture, beat by beat, a little sensuous fire.... (55).

Though most of the words function as nouns, at times some of them are used as verbs, *e.g.*, "She smiled at everybody and *salaamed* me..." (52). Compound words like "*rangoli*-strewn" (65), "*Pan*-red lips" (29). "*tantrik,* rituals" (54), etc. are apt and economical. Apart from these, there are a number of associational words, like *nirvana, bikhus, sadhus, kirtans, prasad, aarati, tantrik, tantras, khir, bhakti, shakti, bhakta, panda, dharmashala, brahma, Rudra, Vishnu, Krishna, Shiva,* etc. which have been put to good use.

Arun Joshi's writing reverberates with the feel of Indian life. His mastery over the treatment of Indian themes, ethos, and culture is effectively correlated by his use of a sensuous and picturesque language. A typical Joshian style is really striking, as the following passage would show :

> Across the steps, in a staggered row, half a dozen men their marvelous oiled bodies faintly gleaming, barrelled through marathon of calisthenics. A young Sanskrit scholar recited hymns at the tope of his voice. I thought of my father and his little book of the Upanishads. Another boy, equally young, corrected him. Did Panini ever live in Benaras? Behind the scholars, two young men, drowned in *bhang*, did a fancy jig. Boatmen, jugglers, vagrants, monkey men, idlers, beggars, flutists, bathers, the watcher of funeral pyres, junkies, medicine men, vendors, each sat in his appointed place, as if on a stage, performing parts that they had performed over the millenia (48).

This is a highly suggestive scene on the ghat of Benaras. The novelist can very vividly capture Indian ethos with the help of powerful images. *The Last Labyrinth* presents an impressive fusion of the novelist's vision of Indian life and philosophy and a fresh Indianized language. The enduring appeal of the novel is due to Joshi's balanced treatment of Indian ethos and Indian English to suit his purpose.

REFERENCES

1. Braj B. Kachru, *The Indianization of English : The English Language in India*, Delhi : OUP, 1983, p. 87.
2. *Ibid.*, p. 131.
3. K.S. Srinivasan, *The Ethos of Indian Literature : A Study of its Romantic Tradition,* Delhi : Chanakya Publications, 1985, p. 2.
4. Quoted in Jugal Kishore Chand, "Commonwealth Literature : A search for Identity", in *Souvenir* on International Seminar on Commonwealth Literature organized by Utkal University, 1991, p. 23.
5. Arun Joshi, *The Last Labyrinth*, Delhi : Orient Paperbacks, 1981, p. 11.
6. B.G. Tilak, *Srimat Bhagavat Gita-Rahasys*, English Trans, by B.S. Sukthankar, Poona : Aryabhushan Press, 1965 rpt., p. 82.

7. Funk and Wagnalls, *Standard Dictionary of Folklore, Mythology, and Legend*, New York : Harper & Row, Paperback, 1984 rpt., p. 598.

8. O.P. Mathur, "Arun Joshi and the Gita", in R.S. Pathak (e.d.), *Indian Fiction in English : Problems and Promises*, New Delhi : Northern Book Centre, 1990, p. 142.

9. Arun Joshi, The *Strange Case of Billy Biswas*, Delhi : Orient Paperbacks, 1986 rpt., p. 192.

10. *Encyclopaedia of Religion and Ethics* Vol. XII, p. 468.

11. Frederick Mayor, *A History of Modern Philosophy,* New Delhi : Eurasia.

12. Dilip Kumar Roy, *The Bhagavad Gita : A Revelation*, Delhi : Hind Pocket Books, 1976 rpt., 5.22.

13. *Ibid.*, 9.24.

14. C.L. Inners, *Chinua Achebe*, Cambridge University Press, 1990, p. 2.

8

Orchestra of Discontent : Som's Quest in *The Last Labyrinth*

M. RAJESHWAR AND B. BRAHMANANDA CHARY

Arun Joshi's fictional forte is the exploration of man's inner life. He plunges into the unfathomable depths of human psyche and brilliantly illumines the subtle ways in which it deals with the onslaughts of disturbance to its balance. His protagonists are easily marked out by their hyper-sensitivity, obsessions, introspection, intellect and unconventional Ways of relating to the world. His fourth novel *The Last Labyrinth* deals with an obsessive and highly sensitive individual, Som Bhaskar, and his grappling with the feeling of emptiness and void at the core of his being. his search for adventure and romance in life and finally his unconscious efforts to come to terms with himself and the world amidst discontent and severe social resistance.

Som Bhaskar has been for a long time troubled by' voids — both internal and external. He confesses : "It is the voids of the world, more than its objects, that bother me. The voids and the empty spaces, within and without."[1] He experiences these voids almost continually : on the occasion of his mother's death. every time an affair ends and even when his daughter is born. The feeling of emptiness does not leave him at peace with himself even for a minute. He goes to bed every night feeling empty and wakes up feeling; empty the next morning. He just docs not know what to fill the emptiness with. He knows that there should be something that can fill this vacuum. He feels his psyche urging him to long for it : "I heard a great threshing of the wind way up in the sky. And it says, I want. I want. I want" (106). When asked to name what he wants he bitterly cries being unable to identify it. Consequently, he experiences sorrows that do not let him breathe. He finds within himself "nothing but an empty roaring, like the roar of the sea in a conch" (115). He fights insomnia all night and sleep-walks through the day. He knows that this is something weird to happen to anybody but he can do nothing about it at the conscious level.

Som has made several unsuccessful attempts to find out what he wants. The enjoyment of money and riches is the first. He has been born into a phenomenally rich family and has had access to every imaginable luxury that money can bu~,. With the spirit of an American tycoon and guided by the dictum 'survival of the fittest' he has tried to acquire wealth and the name and fame that go with it. But the world around him (exemplified by the social worker Mrs. Bedi to whom Som offers a fat gift cheque) seems to value things other than money. Money has thus merely added to his misery. He has tried to drown himself in drink and soothe his nerves with tranquilizers but as soon as their effect wore off the voids would return with a relentless ferocity. He has carried on affairs with innumerable women but each of these affairs has ended in bitterness and frustration. He has married Geeta who is "all that a wife could be" (40) and has had two lovely daughters by her, yet he has "goofed it all up" (40). Family life failed to fulfil his need. He has been to the world's finest universities and equipped himself with knowledge which is amazing. Apart from professing a thorough acquaintance with the Indian religious texts (*The Gita*, the Buddha's sermons, etc.) and Western philosophers (Pascal, Descartes) he can, off hand, reel out information on such complicated scientific phenomena as the structure of the DNA, electron shells, atomic weights, computer circuits, the formation of the earth and the evolution of the life forms on it. But his knowledge has done him "Blessed little good" (129). It has raised more questions than it answered. He is also constantly aware of his father's miserable death due to meloncholia upon failing to find a scientific explanation for the mysteries of the world. The old man happened to start wondering if there is a "First Cause that would explain everything, whose nature might lie behind the natures of all the rest" (27) and slipped into meloncholia still wondering about the expression of whose 'will' is man's life. He had no evidence to believe that life is the expression of the will of the First Cause or God. Som therefore, knows that scientific enquiry will lead him nowhere. He has then turned to psychiatry for an explanation of his problem. The experts have told him that he is insecure (but who is not'?), that he is afraid of death (which is not entirely true), that he is looking for youth (which is plain nonsense) and finally that "psychiatry doesn't allow certain approaches to problems" (74) like Som's. He has then turned to a teacher of philosophy, Leela Sabnis, believing in the powers of her cures of philosophical orientation. He has confronted her with a straight question, "Tell me... What do you think is the matter with me?" (80). Leela Sabnis is given to too much analysis. In answer to his question she has told him that he is too much high strung, that he is a neurotic and compulsive fornicator, that he plays games with the world and that he has built a shell around himself for protection against the feelings of inadequacy. She has tried to help him to reason things through by prescribing Descants. But Som has got nowhere. Leaving her apartment for the last time all that he has heard is "the strumming of great chords way up in the sky, beating the old tattoo : I want. I want. I want" (81). Finally, he had examined the efficacy of faith as a possible answer to his quest, although not directly but through the experience of others. He has seen his mother dying inch by inch of cancer and *Krishna*. His mother "believed Krishna would cure her and flushed her capsules down the toilet. Krishna sat on top of her bureau and smiled and smiled, and smiled until she was dead" (57). In a violent reaction to his mother's irrational belief in Krishna, Som happened to sweep the images of gods aud goddesses off the table in his mother's room. thus once for all rejecting God and faith. His resolve is further strengthened by his grand father for whom anything to do with God was embarrassing; yet he was a happy man. Som learnt early enough that one can be an agnostic and be happy at the same time.

Literary critics of various shades have offered their explanations of Som's quest. It has been hinted sporadically that there is a bit of Meursault (of *The Outsider*) and K (of *Trial*) in Som, and therefore, he finds life absurd and can possibly have no solution to his problem. Sanjay Narasinhaiah diagnoses the major temptation of

Som to his succumbing to "a deep rooted desire to know everything in life, ranging from the outcome of his business shares to the outcome of man's belief in God" and adds that his "tragedy was that anything that Cannot be known or logically conceived did not exist for him. And hence, his mental unrest."[2] Devinder Mohan is of the opinion that Arun Joshi makes the narrator (Som) work out the historical reality within Himself, so that "he defines the fictional voice by visualizing the natural impulse moving towards its own destruction."[3] Devinder Mohan comes closest to naming death as the answer to Som's quest.

These critical opinions have their value in understanding the complex character of Som. Still the question of what Som wants, what is capable of fulfilling him and bestowing peace on him remains not properly and convincingly identified and explained. It his "mental unrest" is a result of his rationality, why is Leela Sabnis happy in spite of professing to be a thorough rationalist? Devinder Mohan is only partially right when he says that Som longs for death. In fact, for Som the feeling of death is like "the embrace of something warm tranquilizing, unrelenting" and he sighs "almost in relief" (144) that it is taking him over. But he has an insatiable hunger for life and its myriad adventurous experiences. At the very point of death he cries out. "Not. now. Not now" (144). Towards the end of the novel he certainly grows to love life. Otherwise he would not carry a gum in the face of a threat to his life from Aftab.

In this paper therefore we wish lo take a fresh look at Som's quest. Som's problem has to be examined in the context of the changed social and psychological realities of modern India. For thousands of years Indians have lived in open spaces. in the lap of nature, enjoying a romantic relationship with it and worshipping deities who are mostly personifications of natural forces. Rapid urbanization and modern rationalistic education in recent times caused a dislocation in the psyche of the educated rich leading to problems of adjustment and to the feeling of rootlessness. The romantic relationship with nature has snapped and this has happened rather too fast.

The collapse of the joint family — an inevitable consequence of urbanization — merely added to the problem. It Led to the relaxation of the hold of tradition on the individual and severely corroded the feeling of security. The middle class and richer sections of Indian society, who showed remarkable alacrity to change with changing times on the economic and educational fronts, found themselves utterly undecided about the ethical, religious, social and personal norms that would not govern them. On the religions front especially, while some of these people continued to uncritically cling to their old beliefs, others found themselves confronted with an irresoluble dilemma between agnosticism and faith.

Som finds himself in this unenviable predicament. He is a rich third generation urban Indian. Apart from inheriting the dilemmas of his class he is specially given to "romanticizing" (189) and therefore, in the light of the knowledge of depth psychology. it can be reasonably assumed that he misses romance in his life, and hence goes all out seeking it in his own neurotic way. The word "romantic" is used here in its broadest sense so as to include passion, danger, adventure, challenge, mystery, death and love for the bygone era. It is significant that the voids that we mentioned earlier, occur to him for the first time in a romantic/historical locale : the Ajanta caves. Analytical experience tells us that Som's unconscious allows his hidden wish to surface when it finds the objective correlative. Som however, cannot identity it but his temperament, characterized by obsessions, self-centeredness. egotism and possessiveness has always fitted into a romantic world. He unconsciously desires to work out his passions in a romantic setting without being checked, analysed and corrected.

Bombay life is too prosaic to afford any romance aud adventure to Som. The people that he associates with or is related to are either analysing and judging (Leela, for example) or forcing him to do or not to do something against his will (Mr. Thapar and Dr. K) or too acquiescent and totally lacking in spirit (Geeta) but exerting passive pressure on him all the same. These people make it impossible for him to be himself. Therefore, when he meets Anuradha, the sprightly woman of the labyrinthine Lal Haveli located in the ancient city of Benaras, he unconsciously identifies that it is she whom he has been longing for all his life. He easily understands that Anuradha is the centre of his romantic interest. The first thing that attracts Som to Anuradha is her antique appearance ; "I had noticed Anuradha like one notices a monument : tall, handsome, ruined .... She did not look clever. She wore costumes of twenty years ago — brocade sari, large gold borders, sleeves up to the elbow, antique jewellery. She was obsolete...." (12). She is dark-eyed, sexy and brings up the images of his childhood before his mind's eye. Everything about her is out of the ordinary, exotic and shrouded in mystery. Lal Haveli where she lives with Aftab of feudal blood and Benaras with its streets filled with danger, death, filth and piety present a vivid contrast to the matter-of-factly built Bombay. The spell of Lal Haveli on him is such that he finds an atavistic instinct reviving in him :

> The issue [shares of Aftab's company] had been there, alive all the time, at the back of my mind. But it had been swamped out : by Lal Haveli, its sounds and colours, the maze of its layout and the maze of the city as I had seen it from The terrace, by the unexpected stirring in me of some long dormant essence of a different kind (42).

The architecture of Lal Haveli and the life within, including Azizum's dance and song recitals for the entertainment of guests, conjure up pictures of life from the now long forgotten past for Som. The chivalry of Aftab's ancestors witnessed by Lal Haveli ages ago and Anuradha's rather unusual past add to the mystery and attraction.

As Som gets closely involved with Anuradha he learns that Anuradha is the "right soul" (meaning the right person that his psychiatrist mentioned) meeting whom would result in peace, even drive one "towards a higher goal" (74) and that she is the woman in whom the worlds of matter and spirit (which Leela talked about on the authority of Descartes) merged to form an enchanting whole.

Possessing Anuradha will present him with a challenge and this is definitely part of the romantic quest of Som. Anuradha is not a free woman nor is she married to Aftab. But she is attached to Aftab, and cannot be easily wrenched away from him. She has lived in Bombay. She has acted in films. She has seen it all. Some cannot dazzle her with the attractions and comforts of the metropolis. Through force or love she has to be won. Som uses both. With almost the vengeful attitude of a medieval tyrant he starts buying the shares of Aftab's company (so as to financially ruin him) and at the same time gets passionately involved with Anuradha.

> ...each meeting, far from cooling my passions, served only to fuel them. I lived on the nourishment of the shades thrown by her naked body under the chromatic shower (121-22).

He clings to her as a child clings to his mother: "...I clung to her. I threw myself, my entire desperate weight, the turbulence of my forty years, on her" (125). She sweet-talks like none of Som's women has ever done: ''I don't want to lose you. I would rather die" (138). Unlike in the case of Geeta and Leela love-making with Anuradha is a very romantic experience if not a highly satisfying one. Som feels as though they

> coupled high above the earth, independent of time and space, like a pair of asteroids, locked in each other's gravity. Silent, unable to communicate except what we communicated through the thrust and push and pull of our bodies, we circled high above the empty cities (107).

Yet, the distance between them docs not seem to diminish. He, therefore, takes her to a Himalayan resort and then to Bombay to be completely absorbed in her.

Just when Som is getting used to the idea of happiness he suffers his second heart attack and Anuradha, his only solace, callously deserts him and goes to Gargi, the deaf-mute godwoman, to enlist God's help in saving Som's life! This is a cheap and worn out third rate Hindi film technique. That apart, "God" has always been a stumbling block in Som's happiness. "God" has robbed him of his mother, made a wreck of his father and now separated Anuradha from him. Earlier on, when he and Anuradha were enjoying their vacation on the mountains "God" happened to fall like a shadow between them aud ruin the peace of his mind:

> I lay awake angry with myself, angrier still at her dragging God into that room which until that moment had been the stage for satisfying my wildest fantasies (127).

Now, he has all the more reason to be angry with Anuradha, God and Aftab (the rival in love). Out of his desperation aud perhaps to fulfil a romantic need for revenge, he now wants to settle scores with Anuradha, Aftab and, yes, God too. But it is not easy. The last batch of share certificates of Aftab's company, the acquisition of which is necessary for his revenge, are tucked away in a mountain top temple where a "divine" flame perpetually burns (reminding one of the snow formation of Shiva's phallus at Amarnath). Som undertakes the arduous and highly risky journey only to be told by his doctor, Kashyap, that Anuradha got Gargi to work a miracle to save his life and promised to give him up for good at the behest of Gargi. Some feels frustrated and angry for such unjust interference of gods and godly people in human affairs. It appears to him as if everyone around him is bent on making him a believer and suggest faith as a solution to his problem. Anuradha, for example, has asserted that "Krishna begins where Darwin left off" (132) and now sends the image of Krishna through Aftab asking him to carry it with him always. Gargi tells him that there is no harm in believing that God exists and that He works in a subtle way (parenthetically one is tempted to ask : how do these people know how God works, if there is one at all'?) Even Dr. Kashyap seems to subscribe to the view that only a miracle has saved Som and not medicine or his will-power. And critics have chimed in and freely• endorsed these views![4] Som. however, rightly finds it absurd to start believing in God in the face of his many deprivations on account of God and the overwhelming evidence to prove that faith is born of a psychological need and that most of the objects of worship are mere natural phenomena (the divine flame worshipped at the said temple is nothing but burning natural gas). In any case, faith has been something that he considered and discorded a long time ago. There is no point in black-mailing him into believing that God or a miracle has saved his life and therefore he should turn pious. He gives all his tormentors a final and fitting reply :

> It is easier to believe that He does not exist. It is more convenient that way... one can't order belief. I must have evidence.... In the absence of evidence I intend to challenge the whole thing (213).

Challenge he does and wins. Back home in Bombay he not only manages to reconcile himself to the demands of life but learns to live without Anuradha and God. He dismisses his reminiscences of Anuradha and impulses towards faith in God as "strange mad thoughts" (223). He knows that faith would have certainly failed, like everything else, to fill his inner void. In spite of his famed faith and equipoise Aftab cannot take hold of himself in the face of traumatic experience — the disappearance of Anuradha — as is evidenced by his incoherent letter to Som :

> I cannot live without her ... endlessly,
> I walk the mazes ... I knock my head against walls ... I am finished (222).

Now, where is the guarantee that faith will have a soothing effect on Som? Som's agnosticism is born of the simple fact that thousands of' years after the idea of God was conceived God still needs to be proved and established. If there were really somebody called God it would not have taken so long to establish Himself beyond a shade of doubt. No useful and real thing ever requires such a long time and so much effort to make itself obvious. It may be true that "There was nothing simple about Krishna. Had it been so, He would not have survived ten thousand years" (173). But the complexity is rather in the minds of the devotees and not with Krishna. It is the weak-willed devotees who keep Krishna alive. Som may have many afflictions but weak will is certainly not one of them.

The restoration of Som to the world seems to occur because of his inner strength, will-power and perhaps the love of his loyal wife. His unconscious urge for romance and adventure has been somewhat satisfied. He is weary but he is relatively at peace with himself. His reconciliation with life is suggested by two subtle devices employed by the author. One, the novel is narrated by Som after having gone through these disturbing experiences. That he narrates the whole story with such clarity and objectivity is proof enough that he has taken stock of himself and has learnt to relate to the world on the basis of love. Two, where earlier he was "mortally afraid of death" (74) he now mocks at death by casually putting a gun to his temple.

REFERENCES

1. Arun Joshi, *The Last Labyrinth* (New Delhi : Orient Paperbacks, 1981) 47. Subsequent page references are to this edition and are parenthesised within the text of the article.
2. Sanjay Narasimhaiah, "Arun Joshi : *The Last Labyrinth,*" *The Literary Criterion* 16.2 (1981) : 82.
3. Devinder Mohan, "The language of the Splintered Mirror : The Fiction of Arun Joshi," *Ariel* 14.4 (October 1983) : 28.
4. For example, the main argument of R.S. Pathak is that Som "is badly in need of a healing touch of an unqualified faith."

   "Human Predicament and Meaninglessness in Arun Joshi's Novels," *The Fictional World of Arun Joshi*, ed. R.K. Dhawan (New Delhi : Classical Publishing Company, 1986) : 136.

   O.P. Bhatnagar argues, "Believe it or not, there exists a world beyond the bounds of reason and science ... The puzzles and contradictions of life cannot but be resolved through faith."

   "The Art and Vision of Arun Joshi," *The Fictional World of Arun Joshi*, ed. R.K. Dhawan (New Delhi : Classical Publishing Company, 1986) : 67.

   Inder Nath Kher observes, "only a Kierkegaardian 'leap of faith' into the spiritual, the Unconscious, the irrational can provide him with a balanced perspective."

   "The Archetypes of Love and Death in Arun Joshi's *The Last Labyrinth,*" *The Journal of Indian Writing in English* 20, 182 (Jan-July 1992) : 59.

9

Race Consciousness in Arun Joshi's *The Last Labyrinth*

SHUBHA TIWARI

Arun Joshi's novel *The Last Labyrinth* is unique in the sense that it demonstrates very clearly inherent patterns of "collective consciousness" and "racial memory" as discussed by Jung and Frazer among psychologists and Northorp Frye, Lestie Fiedler, Miss Bodkin among modern myth critics. India with all her mysticism, ancient religious wisdom, concepts of eternal cycle, sacrifice, caste structure, Krishna and Brahma is strewn all over the novel. Even though the main character of the novel Bhaskar claims to be an atheist, his thinking, mind and voice are full of racial memory. The way Bhaskar talks, and dreams and the way his mind works shows the dark layers of ages of experience over which he has little control. About a good work of art, Carl Jung writes — "We are reminded in nothing of everyday, human life but rather of dreams, high time fears and the dark recesses of mind that we sometimes sense with misgiving"[1]. This stands true for *The Last Labyrinth.*

Awake or asleep, alone or in company, Bhaskar all of a sudden hears the song "I want, I want, want....". "Hunger of the body. Hunger of the spirit"[2] seem to be the central themes of this novel. It is the unsatiable physical and mental thirst of Bhaskar that takes him to Anuradha, to seek the shares of Aftab's company, to Benaras, to Gargi and finally, to Krishna. This hunger is nothing but the present guilt to a race that feels that it originally believed in satisfaction and content rather than hunger for more and more and more. The song "I want I want I want" is not a personal neorosis of the protagonist or the writer but mental guilt of a while race. "The artist is to be freed from the charge that his vision is merely a symptom of some personal psychic maladjustment and from the charge that his symbols are merely subjective distortions."[3] This yarning of Bhaskar "I want, I want, I want" throughout the novel, is explained also at times he is running after fame, women, money and power. He is horribly hungry for all these things and yet he says "I knew that money was dirt, a whore. So were houses, cars, carpets. I knew of Krishna, of the lines he had spoken; of Buddha at Sarnath, under the full moon of July setting in motion the wheel of Righteousness...." It is the combined racial memory which is speaking these words through Bhaskar, a man who is running after the very things he is condemning — money, cars, carpets.

The city of Benaras is again one big enigma of the novel. Bhaskar cannot stand the city, its narrow lanes. its shabby people and its strange traditions. Why, then, he is drawn to Benaras like a magnet to iron. He goes to Benaras again and again. A multi-millionaire of Bombay that he is, he eats pan, walks naked feet, goes to temples and gets in stampedes, draws inspiration from the burning pyres at Manikarnika ghat and so on. He may like it or not, he has a definite realisation of belonging to this most ancient city of the world. This city is the bridge that unites him to his fellow beings. "This city at least, we had in common"[4] He feels that he to "was familiar" with Benaras. Benaras had stirred "in me of some long dormant essence of different kind"[5]. He cannot resist his unconscious mind rushing to him with all its force when he sees the city of Benaras. He does not feel that he has entered a new city. He belongs to the place. All his past memory starts dancing in front of him. "So, this was the city that had been famous before Rome was known or Cyrus had built the Persan Empire...."[6] Pages after pages Joshi's pen flows on the mystery that is Benaras. Manikarnika Ghat reminds Bhaskar of his father and his little book of the Upanishads.[7] When Aftab shows Benaras and Ganga — "He put it as though indicating a personal possession."[8] Bhaskar's mind starts whirling and swooping while sailing through Ganga as though he is crossing Vaitarini itself — "I felt as though this was not Ganga but some unknown stream, in some unknown segment of the universe leading to a reality I had not yet known."[9] The way Benaras annihilates Bhaskar shows the merger of his individual memory in the big ocean of collective memory. "He (the writer) becomes one with us all in the presence of our ancient Gods, the protagonists of fables we thing we no longer believe"[10]. The mysterious lanes at night awake and arouse the unity of minds. The moments of pain, crises, estacy, wonder remind the sensitive soul of the oneness of souls. "The fact is that the nocturnal world is in some sense the world of all of us.[11]

Myth critics say that primitive man still lurks within each of us. The modern man, a man of automobiles, television, computer and internet still "recreates nightly in his dreams the primordial symbols of ancient myth."[12] Archetypal patterns discussed at length by critics include such images as guilt-ridden wanderer, the mysterious cave, fountains, buried grains etc. *The Last Labyrinth* comes very close to these symbols when Bhaskar talks about closed caves of Ajanta where for the first time he consciously linked himself to his racial and wider past. Bhaskar himself comes very close to the image of a guilt-ridden wanderer. Bhaskar again and again visualises himself lost in a dark cave. The dark cave haunts him. He feels "voids of caves and voids of the sky; the terrible vacancies of lokalok". It is a cave of his private and at the same time collective racial fantasies, recurring dreams and obsessive ideas. Jung places these experience above "actual conscious insight"[13]. These recurring nightmares, compulsive behaviour, involuntary crying is Bhaskar's, what Jung calls "psychic energy" because in these experiences lies the key to understand his apparent behaviour. Psychic energy is "the play of opposites"[14] and isn't Bhaskar's mind a play of opposite forces of individual will and ancient latent consciousness. Bhaskar is torn apart between Bombay (modern) *versus* Benaras (ancient), plastics (business) *versus* Krishna (God), Anuradha (mystery) *versus* Geeta (reality). He is a man swinging between the two poles of faith and atheism. Ages and ages of immovable faith does not let Bhaskar rest when he denies the existence of God. Anuradha insists that Bhaskar does not need her. She says this to him even when he is crying helplessly in her arms. Finally, she sends him in search of Krishna and presents him with an icon of Krishna. He needs faith, that is Anuradha's answer to his song — "I want, I want, want...." Even the psychiatrist says that Bhaskar needs religion and faith when he discusses with him his mental complications. The psychiatrist talks about a spiritual solution[15]. Joshi quotes a line from Kierkegard, which I feel can calm the turbulent waters of Bhaskar's mind — "Prayer does not change God but it changes him who prays".

Arun Joshi gives religion an important place at every critical juncture of Bhaskar's life. Religion strikes him when he is most vulnerable. So it is true for all men. Religion commands when someone dies, or marries or is born. Rituals like funeral haunt Bhaskar. Religion, the only rock like reality of life strikes him at every crucial turn of his life. He may ignore religion but within him, he knows that it will strike again some day. Northorp Frye talks about archetypal symbols to which writers compulsively turn. Here, god, rituals, ancient feel are definitely such archetypal symbols, the myth is the central informative power that gives archetypal significance to the ritual and archetypal narrative to flashes of inner illumination.

It is a matter of speculation that this novel gives the reader a familiar feeling. The responses can be easily foreseen by the reader himself. It seems simply obvious that the last labyrinth can be nothing except death. It needs no teaching to tell as to what is the last mystery, the last solution, the final salvation. We know it. When Bhaskar asks Aftab about the last labyrinth, he replies naturally "Why, death, of course".[16] And again one may ask, why this of course. But, we know it, don't we?

Joshi also takes into account the impression of the immediate archetype, *i.e.*, the parents. Joshi has shown the way parents can infect a child's mind with questions. Bhaskar's father is dead but has left with his son, his theory of the First cause. The talk of eternal cycle never actually leaves Bhaskar. His father had said — "Every things happens in cycles. Birth, Growth, Destine and Death."[17] Howsoever, he may detest his mother's undying faith in Krishna. He cannot get rid of the feeling himself. When finally he goes to the mountain temple in search of Krishna, he meets a young boy. The story is touching when we know the young boy's mind has been corrupted by his grandmother. He had been set by the lady in search of a crystal pebble with a star. "The thought depressed me that a child so young should have been contaminated in such a manner. This, too, was corruption, although of a different sort. For all one knew, he would spend the rest of the days searching for a crystal pebble with a star. And become a nut in the process".[18] One cannot deny that restlessness has been implanted in Bhaskar by his immediate past *i.e.*, his parents.

As the novel progresses, the voice of the ancient mythical world gets more and more established. Very little doubt remains. I had heard of people who, staring into....flames and enjoyed the Eternal Bliss....Others had discovered their oneness....with the Brahma. A man I once traveled with — one of the most sophisticated I have ever met — claimed he had seen in such a flame his previous incarnations."[19] This is the voice of inherited wisdom which has a stronger imprint than the voices of the surrounding, actual world. The way Bhaskar prays to God to grant his peace through dead Anuradha sets the supremacy of the racial memory in the novel.

The question arises whether Arun Joshi has been conscious of these inherent undercurrents in the novel. In all probability, he has been. The psychiatrist refers to Carl Jung — "He took out a book from a shelf and read out something. It had touched me, moved me briefly to another plane. The book was by Carl Jung, I bought it later. A scatter of Jung's words passed through my head...."[20] *The Last Labyrinth* with other novels by Joshi, seems to be a conscious effort at depicting unconscious processes. Off and on, Bhaskar seems fully aware of the unknown world that lies within him. He is drawn towards these inner forces magnetically. "I hear the voices of dead people"[21], he says. The death of elders and the awareness of their dead existence burdens the protagonist's already heavily loaded mind. "You walk into your parents house after they are dead and the house starts talking"[22] — it is this approach of the impossibility of escaping the past that gives Joshi's writing the fatalistic tone that it has. The novelist is completely aware of the heavy burden of not only the immediate past but also of the centuries that have gone in shaping an individual. None one pull away from the past nor can deny it. Abut Aftab, Bhaskar thinks "could Aftab get away from the legacy and fill this emptiness with plastic power?" After all, "somewhere behind him, his troubled and fiery past still loomed."[24]

REFERENCES

1. Jung, Carl, *Modern Man in Search of a Soul*, Harcourt, Brace and Company Inc., 182.
2. Joshi, Arun, *The Last Labyrinth*, Orient Paperbacks, 11.
3. Wimsatt, William K. and Brooks Cleanth, *Literary Criticism — A Short History,* Oxford and IBH, 719.
4. Joshi, 55.
5. Joshi, 42.
6. Joshi, 37.
7. Joshi, 48.
8. Joshi, 38.
9. Joshi, 49.
10. Fiedler Leslie, "Archetype and Signature". *The Sewanee Review,* IX, 273.
11. Wimsatt and Brooks, 719.
12. Wimsatt and Brooks, 709.
13. Jung Carl, *Psychology and Religion,* New Haven, 45 — "The unconscious mind is capable at times of assuming an intelligence and purposiveness which are superior to actual conscious insight."
14. Jung Carl, *Modern Man,* 117.
15. Joshi, 74.
16. Joshi, 37.
17. Joshi, 27.
18. Joshi, 186.
19. Joshi, 210.
20. Joshi, 75.
21. Joshi, 68.
22. Joshi, 67.
23. Joshi, 39.
24. Joshi, 40.

10

"Isolation" in Arun Joshi's *The Foreigner* and *The Last Labyrinth*

S.S. RENGACHARI

Arun Joshi's protagonists suffer a strange hunger and the two novels under consideration, analyse the acute mental conflict experienced by them. They go through an agonising sense of isolation and indulge in investigations trying to trace the cause of their unusual mental trauma. They also try to find solutions to their problems.

The characters attempt at first to discover themselves, to recognize themselves and their minds. In the process they question their own attitudes to the happenings around them and their responses to these experiences. They find their predicament similar to being placed between the devil and the deep sea. At heart they wish to yield to their primeval instincts while the other educated self wishes to fulfil the requirements of a modern sophisticated life.

Arun Joshi's first novel, *The Foreigner,* is a presentation of the uprooted hero Sindi Oberoi. Away from his home grounds he regards his past as absolutely meaningless. Life has no hopes for him in the future and he feels that it will be as bleak as the past. 'In this novel Joshi is a contemporary sensibility etching out the inner wasteland of the archetypal modern urban everyman', says Harimohan Prasad [Alienation to Arrival: *The Foreigner* (New Delhi: Arnold-Heinneman, 1985, p. 28)].

Sindi Oberoi, and Som Bhaskar in *The Last Labyrinth* make a deep search for their identity, hoping to arrive at the meaning of life. Sindi is a Kenya born Indian who is unable to find his roots.

He is of mixed parentage and isolation is almost forced on him with the loss of his parents at the age of four. Denied parental love and care in his childhood, Sindi develops an unbearable sense of insecurity. He is an orphan and is afraid he may have to face ridicule. He shrinks into his shell and avoids company with all seriousness.

He is brought up by his uncle and is educated in Nairobi, London and Boston. He grows up to be a sensitive individual and everything seems unreal and transitory. The little he has learned from his uncle and aunt does not satisfy his thirst to learn about his motherland India, and establish his identity. He avers, 'Look at me, I have no roots. I have no system of morality. What does it mean to me if you call me an immoral man. I have no reason to be one thing or another' (*Foreigner*, p. 118). His ancestry is Indian but he grows up in America. He is a foreigner to both the East and the West. He knows next to nothing of the culture to which he belongs and the culture of America where he is brought up makes him feel a sense of isolation from the rest around him.

Sindi's being an Indian has always been a source of embarrassment to him. He says, 'I was born an Indian and had been spat upon; had I been a European, I would have done the spitting' (*Foreigner*, p. 26). His views on love are ridiculed. Expatiating on love he says, 'Love was like a debt that you had to return sooner or later. And if you didn't you felt very uncomfortable' (*Foreigner*, p. 54). He receives very caustic remarks from Karl. He shocks Sindi saying, 'You Indians have got strange theories. One of these days you will all go nuts, I can assure you' (*Foreigner*, p. 54).

The International Students Association arranges a ball to bring about better understanding between the students of America and those of the other countries. But strangely enough, the foreign students did not feel they were welcome there at all. They felt as though it was a charity show. One had 'to go to a public hall, buy a ticket and then search the place for a girl you can dance with...' (*Foreigner*, p. 21). There was then the pretence of being courteous to total strangers and promises to meet again when they knew very well that there was hardly any chance of their meeting again.

Sindi has nothing positive to say about his long years in Boston. He feels that he had spent all his time uselessly. He says, '...twentyfive years largely wasted in search of things in wrong places. Twentyfive years gone in search of peace' (*Foreigner*, p. 80). The only experience he cherishes in his long stay in America is the love and friendship of June Blyth. She is a typical, American, modern girl, but full of love, tenderness and peace. He declines her offer of love because he believes he is 'detached'. He realises his mistake only when June meets with a tragic death. Yet love and life seem to have no significance for him. The only real things for him are birth and death.

Sindi leaves for India soon after the completion of his education. He joins Mr. Khemka's firm. He realises that even his motherland is not free of the avarice for material benefits. He boldly criticises Mr. Khemka to his face. He holds him responsible for his son Babu's death. He discovers that the industrialist maintains double accounts and imaginary records. He is not prepared to support the dishonest practices of the rich man. He tells him categorically, 'You can't label every dirty thing you do as part of the game' (*Foreigner*, p. 178). Sindi is shocked at the chicanery of the Indian businessman and his indifference to the time honoured values like honesty and sincerity. In this respect India does not seem to be any better than the States.

The saving grace in India is the kindness of the traditional Indian girl, Sheila. Like June Blyth, Sheila is full of love and tenderness. He is most at ease in her presence. He has great regard for her intellect, and graceful manners. He admires her willingness to serve her father with a sense of love and devotion. Her genuine regard for him brings them closer. He decides to settle down in life with her. The answer to the isolated soul comes in the form of the young Sheila who makes him realise that love means sharing and caring.

The hero of Joshi's last novel, *The Last Labyrinth* is Som Bhaskar who yearns for peace in life. The labyrinth of life, in which Bhaskar finds himself cornered leads him through untold sufferings. Joshi presents a graphic picture of the hero's pathetic plight. As in *The Foreigner* the scene of action is not one but two places. One is Bombay, the centre of modern life, parallel to Boston in the first novel. The second is Benaras, the seat of Indian tradition, and this city takes the place given to India in *The Foreigner*.

The young multimillionaire Som Bhaskar, has had good Western education, which makes him a supporter of the rational, industrial, technological world. His traditional Indian roots give him a sense of isolation when he is required to follow Western culture in the materialistic world of Bombay. The city has taught him to apply scientific principles to the problems faced by the society but Bhaskar is unable to accept the idea.

Joshi compares and contrasts the sea in Bombay with the life-giving river in Benaras. The comparison is in terms of the impact it has on Bhaskar. In the opening chapter Bhaskar questions, 'Why is the sea so grey here? It is blue down in Goa and bluer still on the coast of Ceylon' (*Labyrinth*, p. 9). The turbulent grey sea symbolises the acute mental conflict suffered by the hero. Bhaskar observes, '...the river [Ganga] was always there, at every turn, disappearing momentarily from view only to reappear in a grander vista' (*Labyrinth*, p. 29). The river seems to be a life-giving force to the people living by its banks. On the other hand the sea in Bombay has a charm that produces a soporofic effect. Although Bhaskar recognizes and realises the power of the river, he is not prepared to accept it so easily. When Aftab proudly takes him to the river, the sceptic in Bhaskar avers, the 'river might have produced poets and saints, even kings, but could they have produced an industrialist?' (*Labyrinth*, p. 39). He rates Bombay superior to Benaras in that it is replete with brilliant industrialists. Benaras is only an ancient city of historical value to him and further, it is often infested with dacoits. But Bhaskar feels that he experiences a sense of isolation and loneliness in both the places. Both are thickly populated but neither of them is able to give him the sense of belonging he craves for and rid him of his unbearable, inexplicable sense of isolation.

Bhaskar, in spite of all his misgivings about Benaras, is charmed by Lal Haveli. It is here that he gets to know Anuradha who means much to him as a source of his mental peace. Yet he has his own misgivings about Benaras and considers Lal Haveli 'a tawdry, sensual den, a dead house in a dead city' (*Labyrinth*, p. 108).

Bhaskar's quest in life is to find out why he should believe in the mystic concepts of Indian tradition. His search does not lead him to any positive conclusion. His father has voiced his doubts about the 'First Cause' in his son's presence. The father's intention is to discover the connection between cause and effect. His grandfather on the other hand was a lover of a luxurious life and a pleasure seeker. The grandson was exposed to these two contradictory attitudes at home, at a very early age. It is this lack of stability in the formative stage at home that has led to such an anxiety in life. The traditional views are learnt by an ordinary Indian as a child and he realises — their significance as he grows up in life. This advantage is denied to the children of wealthy Indian families in Joshi's novels. In the name of freedom and modernity the child has been forced to fend for himself where important issues like religious beliefs are concerned. He feels the insecurity of one in a rudderless boat right from childhood. No amount of material prosperity can give the child the secure sense of identity he feels with his own people.

With all his unpleasant habits of boozing and womanising, Bhaskar is able to retain his wife Geeta's heart for himself. While Aftab, Anuradha and Gargi advocate 'faith', Geeta lives it in her life. Bhaskar no doubt admires her tenacity of purpose and sincerity as his wife, but he is unable to understand her. His mental conflict is caused by various factors pertaining to the scientific, materialistic, sensual as well as the spiritual. Geeta judges him accurately and fulfils his needs while Bhaskar is not even able to judge himself. Her traditional sense of devotion and duty makes him look on her as an angelic personality.

The Joshian heroes face a conflict that is common to the entire world of sceptics. They cannot feel at home in their own tradition because they have only learnt to question and not to analyse the profound values that lie hidden behind traditional practices. They are not satisfied with the modern knowledge they have accumulated because it does not give them a substitute for the concepts they debunk. They find themselves isolated even in a crowd.

11

Symbol as Structure : Arun Joshi's *The City and The River*

K.M. PANDEY

The paper discusses the basic symbolism of *The City and the River* which grows out of the structure of the novel. The novel is polysemic in nature and there are obviously layers of meaning and levels of interpretation in it. I intend to proceed by the syllogistic method analysing in the first part the novel as the parable of the times. The second part discuses the localised circumstances that man creates for himself and ultimately gets entangled in. The third part discusses the social dimensions of the novel and analyses the thorough inability and limitless limitations of human beings. All that human beings think and do for themselves under myths of progress and evolution comes at last to nothing. The river consumes the existence of the city in order to make room for the play of God who enjoys himself by creating another course of events and ideas that we call civilization. The fourth part puts up the findings together and makes necessary generalizations that are warranted. The main focus remains upon the impossibility of being and the being of impossibility.

I

The plot of the novel revolves round the story of the city by the river which is ruled by the Grand Master who is visited by a dream in which he sees himself as the king of the city but surrounded by boatmen ready to attack him. He asks his Astrologer to interpret the dream who informs him that "there exists a prophecy that speaks of the coming of a king."[1] Determined to be the king of the city, the Grand Master, at the advice of the Astrologer, introduces "The Era of Ultimate Greatness" (23) which has the "Triple way" or the Way of Three Beautitudes" that means the implementation of his tyranny in the city. However, the headman of the boat people who is a woman, does not agree to abide by the new rules made for the city.

The new era is inaugurated with the arrest of a boatman and a clown who had laughed at the Grand Master. The incident fills the citizens with "fear and foreboding" (23). Later, when Bhumiputra, better known as Master Bhoma, who teaches Mathematics at the University, is arrested but does not reach jail and is also not found; his teacher, known as the Professor, takes up the responsibility of finding him out. He is assisted in his search forthwith by a ten year old nameless child whom he calls his Little Star. The police report tells him that a group of armed men attacked the jeep and, after a short scuffle, carried the prisoner away which proves Bhoma's involvement in an outrageous conspiracy against the Grand Master. The people of the city also do not believe in the report and feel angry.

When the Grand Master goes on his night watch, he hears a music coming from the river. He hates music, so at his orders, all the musical instruments of the boatmen are destroyed. In such an atmosphere of awe and terror comes the Festival of the Great River. Again there is the boat race but this time the boatmen are not allowed to race barebodied. They have to wear sport-shirts supplied by the Astrologer and they have also to salute the Grand Master. The problem is that they do not "know how to salute a man, be he a Grand Master" (90). So they have to practise it which arouses anger in them.

At the Festival the Astrologer performs a *Yajna* "in the tongue that no one understood" (96) in which he substitutes the hymn of the great river with another composition that speaks of the greatness of kings and their indispensability to the earth. At this the Hermit of the Mountain, who had been his fellow disciple at the cottage of Great Yogeshwara, stands up in anger and informs the Astrologer in the same tongue that he has committed sarcrilege. After the Hermit's departure the son of the Grand Master is crowned and the public is asked to cheer him up but there is very cold response because "the multitude was either confused or unwilling" (102). Soon Dharma, the Professor, and hundreds of boatmen are arrested and sent to the gold mines because their lips had not moved during the oath taking ceremony after the coronation of the Son. The Master of Rallies, who is an important member of the Grand Master's Advisory Council, is also to be jailed because of his failure to present live telecast of the programme. To avoid the torture he commits suicide.

Meanwhile, the commissioner of the city hatches a conspiracy under which he gets the photograph of about fifty sturdy young boatmen armed with spears, daggers, bows and arrows, and with this photograph he proves his vigilance in the city for which the Grand Master elevates him to "the Rank of the Minister for Trade" (119). And the final report proves Bhoma to be a great conspirator who has many ring leaders as his followers.

The Professor knows that all the reports about the conspiracy are fake and decides to tell the truth to the people. He begins a free lottery Stall for this purpose. The winner of this lottery is handed a boquet of flowers. But his bare facts do not attract good gathering. Later, a lean and thin boy, who is identified as Shailaja's brother and Bhoma's student, comes forward to tell the truth through fiction — through the fable of the king who became naked and exposed. But the lottery stall is also destroyed; the flowers are crushed; and the Professor is jailed. When the headman of the boatpeople takes up the Professor's mission, she is also arrested and sent to the Gold Mines. Despite many kinds of torture she does not accept the Grand Master's rules. She tells the Astrologer, my reply is as before. "I spit on you and I spit on the Grand Master" (164). In turn, her eyes are gogued out and the Professor goes on a fast. He dies in the gold mines expecting "a new world" (167).

The Professor's death makes Bhoma very sad and one night he sees an oarless boat and immediately knows what he has to do. Getting into the boat he reaches the boatmen and tells them the parable of the king who became naked and exposed. The boatmen take a pledge that "there would be no movement on the river until their oppressor opened his eyes and ears to their lament" (179).

Meanwhile, the Minister for Trade and the Education Advisor involve them in another conspiracy to oust the Grand Master and grab the power for themselves. They also decide to assist the boatmen with the shock brigades of the Education Advisor. Despite Bhumiputra's advice the boatmen accept the unconditional alliance of the shock brigades. Consequently, "schools, shops, telephone exchanges and railway stations are systematically burnt" (182) and the very next night the gold mines are broken and all the prisoners are set free. But during the following night two hundred sleeping boatmen are brutally killed and thrown into the river. This obviously leads to open clashes between the boatmen and Grand Master's forces. Shailaja's brother is so much shocked by the brutal killings that he commits suicide. The Hermit of the Mountain performs a *yajna* for the peace of the departed souls. He gathers the boatmen on the bank of the river and recites some *mantras* to correct the wrong done by the Astrologer on the inaugural day of the New Era. He realises the truth of the prophecy and knows that the end of the city is imminent. Soon the river consumes the whole city barring one child so that he may tell the truth in future.

II

With Arun Joshi symbol is not merely a stylistic device; it is the formative principle which governs the narrative pattern and the presentation of character in his novels. Each of his novels is on aesthetic working out some symbolic motif. *The City and the River* is no exception. The title symbolizes the juxtaposition of two opposite forces — one manmade and the other natural. The novelist unequivocally suggests that this opposition is not permanent and the possibility of reconciliation between the two is always there, but it is the city which has to reconcile with the river because the city evolves out of the river, and not the river from the city.

The way the city has been built up is symbolic. It begins with "the narrow brown band of mud huts" (12). Next, on a higher ground, is "the neat rosy pink oval of the brick colonies and their special schools, clubs, shopping arcades" (12). Beyond them are the famous Seven Hills which are the seat of the Grand Master's government. On the tallest hill stands the palace of the Grand Master. Beyond these hills are the pyramids and in the far distance are some snow-covered peaks which have not yet been scaled. "No one as yet climbed the mountain even though, for hundreds of years men have launched expeditions against it and two hundred men have died in the attempt" (12-13). The hierarchical division of the city into mud houses, brick colonies and the palace symbolizes the division of the city according to the power acquired by the people who inhabit these houses. In the city the Grand Master has secured the highest place but there are still higher places where he aspires to go. This symbolizes man's attempt to climb up higher and higher in the Great Chain of Being[2]. The Virgin peaks of the mountain, however, symbolize man's inability to attain godhood without the help of God.

The palace of the Grand Master is situated on the Seven Hills which symbolizes the seven lands of knowledge described in the *Upanisadas.* The fearful dream of the Grand Master implies the Grand Master's fear from the boatmen because dreams are, as Freud says, the expression of unfulfilled desire and fears through "the unconscious mind wherein lurk and moil basic impulses of the race and also thwarted personal desires."[3]

The river is not monolithic in nature. It symbolizes different things to different people. To the Grand Master it is simply the flow of water which can have only material value. Blinded by his power he cannot visualize that water can purify, regenerate and also destroy; because the loss of vision and the death of intuition have turned him into a robot which can function only mechanically. He is still capable of hearing the music of the river but instead of soothing him it only estranges and antagonises him. He destroys the musical instruments of the boatmen — the children of the river — because they sing songs in her honour. To the boatmen the river is everything. Without her they have no existence. They are like fishes — active, alive, happy and gay when they are near her; but away from her their lives have no meaning. "They consider themselves to be the children of the river, and to the river, and river alone, do they hold allegiance" (14). The Astrologer tells the Grand Master that "the river for them ... is a symbol of divine mother. Of God Himself" (22). She is to the boatmen what Nature is to William Wordsworth — "the nurse/The Guide, the guardian of my heart, and soul/of all my moral being".[4]

The river looks after her children and chooses persons to be her interpreters. The river is also symbolic of the Great Trinity of Brahma, Vishnu and Mahesh in the Indian religion. Like Brahma, she has created the city; like Vishnu, she provides sustenance to it; and like Shiva or Mahesh, she goes on taking the poison for the well-being of the city, but when angry, she also destroys the city. When Shailaja's brother, one of her true sons, burns his own pyre, the people of the city notice that "upstream the river too had caught fire. The glow of the burning river lit up the mangroves and the mud-huts" (228-29). After the continuous rain of seven days and seven nights the water of the river enters the city. When the son of the Grand Master attacks the rose farm which sheltered the man [Master Bhoma] who had risen from the river (257), the river turns very furious. The river comes forward to punish the evil doers. Consequently, "there was nothing but boiling leaping water as far as the eye could see" (257). The death of the city is symbolic in two ways : it emancipates the true sons of the river from endless and unbearable suffering; and it punishes their oppressors.

The whole city is drowned in the fury of the river but as she is the universal mother of the city she knows that people will again come to her to live by her, and in due course there would be another grand master more tyrannous than the one whom she has recently killed. The city will, then, need a *Jnani*, obviously to be another hermit, who will lead the people to the path of righteousness; so the river selects one child who had been illegitimate in the eyes of the city but to her eyes seems to be the most pious child. The river takes the child on the oarless boat and saves him. The child and the boat are the archetypes of Noah's ark in the Great Flood[5], when the whole of the earth was covered with water and all creatures, except those on the ark, were destroyed. The oarless boat also symbolizes the mantrik body that cannot be destroyed and only a pious soul can enter it.

The characters of the novel are also symbolic. Yogeshwara means "god of the yogis". One becomes a yogi when one has self-control through meditation the purpose of which is to produce mystical experience and the union of the individual soul with the universal spirit. In the novel Yogeshwara is really the god of the Yogis[6] — the Hermit, the Professor, Bhumiputra, the Little Star and, of course, the boatmen. It seems that it is he who is instrumental in sending the mystic oarless boat to help the votaries of truth. The Hermit is "a person living in solitude". He is also a Yogi and the direct disciple of Yogeshwara. He is the seer of the truth which he transfers to his disciples. The Professor is "a public teacher of high rank, especially holder of a chair in University". His duty is to initiate his students to find out truth and with the help of truth to find out the essential meaning of life. The Professor whose name is deliberately not mentioned in the novel, justifies his post. He even sacrifice his life to find out the truth and to tell it to others. His fast unto death symbolizes man's search for new world order to substitute the existing world order. As the voluntary death of John the Savage in Aldous Huxley's *Brave New World*[7] symbolizes his rejection of the rules made by the makers of the new world and his victory over his adversaries, so the Professor's death is also symbolic of his victory over the Grand Master and his forces.

Bhumiputra means "the son of the soil" and he proves himself to be faithful to the land he has been brought up in. Little Star is the name given to the nameless boy by the Professor. The name is symbolically evocative because the Little Star enlightens all those who come into his contact.

He seems to be the Bala Yogeshwara (Child god of the Yogis) who can "see into the life of things."[8] He is simply a ten year old boy but in the case of enlightened men age does not matter[9].

He tells the Professor, "I am thousands of years old ... Everyone is thousands and thousands of years old, tied as we are to the wheel of Karma. Unfortunately, we forget this. Kings and grand masters forget this the most. That is the world's misfortune" (42). The term. Grand Master is also symbolic. It symbolizes that the rulers of the city take it for granted that they are representatives of God upon the earth and the laws made by them are the laws of God. The Astrologer is one who foretells the fortunes of others on the basis of the influence of stars on individual human beings or a country. In the novel, though the Astrologer occupies the chair and also knows the prophecy, he is unable to foretell the truth to the Grand Master. He conveys only partial truth which ultimately leads to the destruction of the city.

III

Typical themes in Indian English Fiction are said to be "the caste system, social attitudes, social and religious taboos, superstitions, notions of superiority and inferiority."[10] To this list may be added myths, legends and fables which also form part of the socio-cultural ethos and philosophical heritage of India. Joshi makes a unique symbolic amalgamation of most of these Indian themes especially the caste system and the notions of superiority as prevalent in the country. If we make a binary division of the struggle in the novel, it is the oppressor *versus* the oppressed or the high caste *versus* the low caste. The Grand Master, the Astrologer, and the key persons in the army are people who hail from high castes. There are two most prominent disciples of Yogeshwara. Both are equally efficient, and in some ways the Hermit is better than the Astrologer because he can utter truth when it is most needed; but the high caste disciple with the sacred thread becomes the Astrologer of the Grand Master and the other disciple remains a hermit who has a small following. The commissioner of the city is "a low caste but competent", so his services are utilized by the Grand Master though he has no respect for the commissioner. The Grand Master grows "used to him, even fond of him as one grows fond of one's dog" (79) which symbolizes the Grand Master's self-assumed superiority over the commissioner. When the struggle between the boatmen and the Grand Master's forces is simmering, the shock brigades of the Education Advisor assist the boatmen "to inflict maximum damage on the commissioner who was not only the strong arm of the palace but also a low caste and an upstart" (182). In the struggle between the Grand Master's forces on one side and the boatmen and the shock brigades on the other, the former lose the battle. "In frustration, they turned their fury on other targets, one such being the famous 'Great River Boats' which belonged to Dharma's father-in-law" (183) who is also a low caste.

The problem is not so simple as it appears to be at the first glance. The society is further sub-divided into higher and lower castes. There are many low castes in the upper castes. Likewise, there are numerous higher castes in the lower castes. Deeply involved in this problem the commissioner tells the Professor :

> The way this high and low business is tearing this city apart, Professor, is truly sad. Sad, and in my case, unfair. These people do not realise that there are thousands of the low whom I too look down upon. I am not a cobler or a boatmen or a pimp or a thousand other things. But these people do not realise this. Just because the Education Advisor is the high of the high he refuses to note that there are hundreds with whom I, too, do not eat, with whom I do not drink, who dare not look at my wife and daughters. But this little understanding is beyond the high brains. To him you are high of the high or dirt. He does not even bother to hide what he thinks. And it hurts. It is all very sad, very unfair (81).

But when the Grand Master makes him the Minister for Trade, he makes an alliance with the same Education Advisor to oust the Grand Master. He does all this to be the next Grand Master. This symbolizes the conflict of Structures. When there is perpetuation of sinful heirarchy, one structure emanates from the other to challenge it, and ultimately leads to the birth of another which will challenge the latter in due course of time. If no structure is able to justify itself, the city is bound to be unreal and inevitably destroyed. The absence of structure means the prevalence of anarchy in the city; and when anarchy prevails, the city is bound to be destroyed either by the internal forces struggling with one another, or by any external force.

IV

"The world belongs to God ... Let Him be the king of what is His" (70) seems to be the message of the novel which manifests the relevance of God to man's choices. Joshi symbolically tells us that God created all creatures but man jumped up very high in the Great chain of Being . Since he possessed intellect, he assumed himself to be the monarch of the world which was the creation of God. This discrimination did not stop at the level of bifurcating man from other creatures. Man continued discriminating against other human beings in the same vein. This resulted in the fragmentation of the human society into different groups. Man started creating circumstances in which he wanted to live. The two disciples of Yogeshwara choose two rather opposite paths[11] for themselves : the Astrologer becomes the destiny maker of the city whereas the Hermit identifies himself with the river and this choice obviously makes them enemies. Both of them interpret the old prophecy about the coming of a king but both interpret it in slightly different manner and they quarrel over a minor variation of it. The most significant part of the prophecy — the destruction of the city — is overlooked by both of them. This is told to them by their common teacher who says : cities, my children, even as men — make their own horoscopes. It is an indication to both of them to interpret the prophecy in relation to the city but they both fail to do it at that time.

The novel does explore the possibility of man's choice between allegiance to God and allegiance to man or, to put it differently, between religion and politics. Those who are weak are easily led to transfer their allegiance from God to man. They do so to pursue their selfish ends and ultimately are trapped in the same net they have created for the fulfilment of their ambitions. They make political use of language which "is designed to make lies sound truthful and murder respectable and to give an appearance of solidity to pure mind."[12] Naturally, they use high-sounding words in inflated style which is a kind of euphemism. "Thus, political language has to consist largely of euphemism, question-begging and sheer cloudy vagueness. Defenceless villages are bombarded from the air, the inhabitants driven out into the country-side, the cattle machine-gunned, the huts set on fire with incendiary bullets. This is called *Pacification*. Millions of peasants are robbed of their farms and sent trudging along the roads with no more than they can carry this is called *transfer of Population* or *rectification of frontiers*."[13] The Grand Master introduces the "Triple way" for the development of the city but this simply means the killing of poor, helpless, honest and innocent boatmen. "The Era of ultimate Greatness" plainly means the spread of awe and terror in the city. The Minister for Trade makes an underhand dealing with the Education Advisor to oust the Grand Master from the power and to acquire it for himself; this is called "A Deed of National Partnership". It does not mean that politicians never use plain and simple language. When they are alone or with those who are their close allies, they speak in clear, unambiguous terms. When the Astrologer shows his fear of God, the Grand Master tells him: "And God — what is God? Does he even exist? He must surely have other things to worry about than intervene in the affairs of this city where we in any case now rule (219).

But the 'headman' has firm faith in God. She asks the Astrologer, "you think an ant is born on this earth without God's will?"(19). The Hermit of the Mountain is sure that the world is the manifestation of God's power upon this earth. He tells the Minister for Trade, "the world belongs to God, Minister. Let Him be the king of what is His .... God is the highest Truth as it is known to each one of us"(70). God helps His devotees whenever they are in trouble. But the question of the periodic destruction of man and his civilisation remains to be a significant one. Yogeshware is sure about the possibility of man's freedom from the bondage of cycles. His parting words to the Nameless One proclaim it :

> "... The main thing is to prevent this endless repetition, this periodic disintegration. But to achieve this we need purity."
>
> "Purity?"
>
> "Yes, the city must purify itself if it is not to dissolve again."
>
> "Purify itself of what?"
>
> "of egoism, selfishness, stupidity."
>
> "But how shall I succeed where the Hermit failed?"
>
> "The question is not of success or failure, the question is of trying. And it is not your success that we are speaking of but the city's. The city must strive once again for purity. But purity can come only through sacrifice. That perhaps was the meaning of the boatmen's rebellion" (262-63).

This preaching obviously based on the *Karma Yoga* of *The Gita* is the vision offered by the novel. G.S. Amur is right when he says that "as an affirmation of India's wisdom (the introduction of Yogeshwara is not fortuitous) and the value of the fable as a mode of comprehension, it [*The City and the River*] has a unique place in Indian Fiction in English."[14] But he expresses his doubt about the future of Arun Joshi as a novelist — "where can he [Joshi] go from here?" The answer to this question is now quite clear but probably Joshi knew that after this novel he had to go nowhere else but to the Abode of Great God.

The philosophic vision of the novel focuses on how man creates and goes on creating, objects that he enjoys as things within a certain periphery that he calls the city. However, in the long run, the city which has become a symbol of growing civilization, comes to mean nothing but a place of corruption committed not only by hegemonic powers but also by those very people who inhabit the city. To all corruptions committed, Joshi suggests, stands a corrective principle which in the novel is symbolized by the river and the people who live by it. So, the novel offers a kind of moral judgment that the city connot exist apart from, or in opposition to, the river for it is the city that has emerged out of the river and not *vice versa*. All cities are artificial for that is what possibly they could be if one is to believe Michel Foucault. And man cannot but build the city as a measure of his mental, social and economic power. This, however, remains a dream for man cannot, in fact has not been, throughout history, able to contain within the confining walls of the city. It is this impossibility of being to manifest within the *enclosures* of the city that he goes to the river. And the moment he goes to the river the city is destroyed which focuses upon the basic dichotomy with which we began : that the novel portrays the impossibility of being and the being of impossibility.

NOTES AND REFRERENCES

1. Arun Joshi, *The City and the River*, New Delhi Vision Books, 1990, p. 15. All the subsequent quotations are from this edition.
2. Arthur O Lovejoy, *The Great Chain of Being.*
3. Joseph T. Shipley, *Dictionary of World Literary Terms,* London : George Allan and Unwin Ltd. 1955, p. 328.
4. *Lines Composed Above Tintern Abbey*, 11.109-11.
5. "And every living substance was destroyed which was upon the face of the ground, both man and cattle, and the creeping things, and the fowl of the heaven; and they were destroyed from the earth, and Noah only remained 'alive', and they that 'were' with him in the ark", "Genesis", 7, 23.

6. *Yoga* has been variously defined. *The Gita* says that excellence in action is yoga (योग: कर्मसु कौशलम्). It also says that to be disinterested in the result of the action is to follow yoga (सिद्धयसिद्धयो: समो भूत्वा समत्वं योग उच्यते). *Patanjalyogasutra* defines it as control over human feelings (योगश्चित्वृत्ति निरोध:).

7. *Brave New World*, New York : Bantom Books, 1939, 33rd rept. 1966. See chapter 18, pp. 164-77.

8. *Tintern Abbey*, 1.49.

9. न तेजसां हि वय: समीक्ष्यते।

10. Braj B. Kachru, *The Indianization of English: The English Language in India*, Delhi : OUP, 1983, p. 87.

11. *Kathopanishad* says that *shreya* and *Preya* both come to people. Enlightened people go for the former and ignorant select the latter path.

    श्रेयश्च प्रेयश्च मनुष्यमेत: तौ सम्परीत्य विविनक्ति धीर:

    श्रेयो हि धीरोऽभि प्रयेसो वृणीते प्रेमो मन्दो योगक्षेमादवृणीते।

    Kath 26, in *Astādasi* : *Isādi Astādasopanisadānam Sārah*. Varanasi : Sarva Seva Sangh Prakashan, 1983 (Second edition), p. 164.

12. George Orwell, "Politics and the English Language" in *20th Century Literary Criticism* ed. David Lodge, Longman, 1972 : rpt. 1992, p. 369.

13. *Ibid*. p. 366.

14. *Indian Literature*, 144, xxxiv, 1991, New Delhi : Sahitya Akademy, pp. 156-57.

12

The Problem of Alienation and the Quest for Identity in Joshi's Novels

S.P. SWAIN AND S. SAMARTRAY

The fictional world of Arun Joshi postulates the clash between alienated self and the socio-cultural forces. The protagonists of his novels are subjected to extreme social, cultural and psychological pressures. The inter-generational tensions engendered with the changing ethos make increasing demands on the individual and contribute in creating a void which is nothing but a chaotic feeling of rootlessness in life, incessantly haunting their psyche and corroding every sphere of their life. This awareness of rootlessness and consequential anxiety is the keynote of Joshi's existential vision of the plight of modern men. The protagonists discover the meaning and value of life probing through the dark mossy labyrinths of the soul. This search for identity is the leitmotif of Arun Joshi's novels.

Joshi's protagonists are confused men who find themselves participating in a wild rat race with no clear goal in mind. The economic drudgery, social pressures, the dissolution of old faiths and dogmas and uncertain loyalties mercilessly crumples their life and wounds their psyche. So they adopt a cynical attitude towards life and the established social norms and values.

They rebel against the socio-cultural pressures and pursue their quest for identity. Through self-probing and self-exploration, through perceptions of the past and alienating experiences of the presents they discover the higher values of life.

Alienation in Joshi's novels stems from a clash between the socio-cultural and psychological forces. The urge for alienation arises out of social maladjustment and emotional insecurity. Incertitude leads to the quest for identity which is a psychic revolt on the pert of the alienated self. This "quest motive" operates more on the socio-psychic plane than on the metaphysical plane. The quest attains spiritual dimensions at certain levels. "My novels", says Joshi, "are essentially attempts towards a better understanding of the world and of myself" .... (Reply to M.R. Dua, dt. September 3, 1971, qtd. R.K. Dhawan). Joshi was influenced by Albert Camus and other existentialist writers : "I did read Camus and Sartre, I liked *The Plague* and read *The Outsider*. I might have been influenced by them" (Interview with Bannerji, *The Sunday Statesman*, qtd. Dhawan).

In *The Foreigner*, Arun Joshi presents Sindi Oberoi as a confused man, a product of diverse cultures. His mixed parental blood and up-bringing in an alien country instils in him a sense of rootlessness. Devoid of a spiritual and cultural anchorage, and being brought up in a loveless world, he harbours in him a deep sense of insecurity and unreality. Against this cultural background Sindi cultivates a sense of detachment to overpower the sad experiences of life. He is a self-deceiver, detached with a sense of delusion.

He even avoids marriage because he is afraid of all familialties : "I was afraid of possessing anybody and I was afraid of being possessed and marriage meant both" (106). His parentage and early life made him the nowhere man.

Sindi's alienation is of the soul and not of geography. He comes to India in search of his ancestral roots. But he fails to carve out a niche for himself. He finds himself as good as a foreigner in India as in America. He realises that his foreignness lay within him : "... my foreignness lay within me and I would not leave myself behind wherever I went" (61) . Rootless end alienated Sindi becomes quite cynical and detached. Gradually he realises that detachment does not mean an escape or isolation but it means devotional sacrifice and involvement. Sindi asserts his identity by fixing his goal in life and settling down to a domestic life in India with Sheela. Dr. Hari Mohan Prasad observes "From Boston to Delhi has been a tourney from alienation to arrivals from selfishness to sacrifice, from an anomie responsible to himself to a member of mankind, from being to becoming" (*Indian English Novelists* 51). From 'detachment to involvement' constitutes the odyssey of Sindi's search for identity.

The search for identity in *The Strange Case of Billy Biswas* assumes a spiritual dimension. It is born out of the socio-cultural clashes to which Billy is subjected. Although Billy belongs to a highly placed bourgeois society with good ancestral background, he feels stifled. He is alienated from the higher middle class society in which he is nursed and nurtured. He suffers from acute social alienation and he cannot identify himself with the society to which he belongs. He often wondered: "Who was I ? Where had I come from ? Where was I going" (23).

The artificiality and pretentions of the bourgeois society are repulsive to him. In a psychic revolt against the existing social norms, he intends to discard his family. He feels a strong force, urkraft .... a primitive force" (101), a deep attraction towards primitivism and the unpretentious life style of nomads. This force compels him to leave his family and seek refuge in the Satpura hills. The natural beauty of Bilasia charms him and he feels a deep satisfaction after his physical union with her. The primitive life style suits him but his search for the higher values of life does not end. "Billy is a refugee from civilisation" (140). He says "Layer upon layer was peeled off me until nothing but my primitive self was left trembling" (121). Such a feeling irks him. He could not rest. His search for identity is more than a psychological process. It is a spiritual quest. Billy says to Romesh : "Becoming a primitive was only a first step, a means to an end. Of course I realised it only after I ran away. I realised that I was seeking something else" (189). This search for the higher values of life becomes the crux of Billy's life but is cut short by his tragic end.

In *The Apprentice*, Joshi portrays Ratan Rathor as a young man from an impoverished middle class family. He has to find his own way and pay his own price in this world. With his mind full of idealism and patriotic fervour, Ratan steps into the arena of job hunting only to be disappointed again and again. To Ratan, it was money that "brought respect and brought security. Money made friends, money succeeded where all else failed. There were many laws .... but money was law into itself" (20). He mortgages his intergrity and idealism for money and a position in society. As he acquires wealth and power, his personality disintegrates and his conscience reels and groans under the weight of his sins. His dying conscience pricks him but he does not give in. The tussle between idealism and morality on the one hand and the craze for money and career on the other creates a void in his psyche. He wants to extricate his identity from the heap of corruption but fails. The ghastly death of his friend, the Brigadier, shakes him out of his moral inertia. He confesses to Himmat Singh : "... There are many sorrows in the world but there is nothing in this world to match the sorrow of a wasted life" (140). In this novel Joshi portrays the most acute kind of self-alienation.

Ratan wants to free himself from the shackles of a valueless urban civilization. Hence, his search for his identity in doing humble and humiliating jobs like shining the shoes at the temple door. His is the spiritual quest for a clean and healthy mind. His repentance and his penance help him to realise his self-identity in this disintegrating world.

Joshi's *The Last Labyrinth*, probes into the turbulent inner world of an industrialist Som Bhasker whose Indian cultural background and foreign education are at perpetual war with each other. A close scrutiny of his personality reveals insecurity and hollowness which propel him from one goal to another. He is relentlessly driven by undefined hungers — hunger for money, hunger for fame, hunger for Anuradha's body and a hunger for some spiritual sublimity.

He tells Anuradha : "I'll tell you what is wrong... I am dislocated. My mind is out of focus. There is something sitting right in front of me and I cannot see it" (107). This something is his other identity, his philistine self. All his life Som has sung the strident song, "I want, I want" (11). This search for the higher values of life involves many probings into the haunted labyrinth of the psyche. Unaware of the nature of his wants he hankers after Aftab's shares. The spiritual influence of Gargi is like balm to his wounded soul but he refuses to accept her spiritual guidance. Som's dilemma is the predicament of the modern man. Born out of the diverse cultural influences his problems disturb him. The Western world of science and rationalism, the Indian world of faith and transcendentalism contribute to his already confused mind. He is completely alienated from his self and gropes about in his search for identity. His mind is like a labyrinth where there are mazes. At length, he realises the futility of his running after wealth. Anuradha's disappearance leaves him psychologically and emotionally wounded. In sheer desperation he cries out :

> Anuradha, If there is a God and if you have met him and if He is willing to listen then Anuradha, my soul, tell Him, tell this God to have mercy upon me. Tell Him I am of so many fears, so much doubting (223).

The novel according to K.R. Srinivasa Iyengar, is a delineation of the pestilent-stricken modern world where people have lost their sense of identity. It is

> a paradigm of the contemporary diseased world where discontents grow their own pestilential vapours, and self-doomed humanity — lacking faith, lacking Grace — is tragically resigned to being suffocated by them in the 'Last Labyrinth' (*Indian Writing in English*: 243).

Joshi's latest novel, *The City and the River* treats the predicament of his characters in a hostile milieu. The crisis of the individual is replaced by the socio-political crisis of the city which represents the whole community. It is the symbol of the collective identity of the mass. The words of the professor reveal a feeling of hopelessness : "God gave me life that I might serve this earth : I have squandered it on a bauble" (163). In a relentless search for their identities, they withdraw from human ambience to natural environs of peace and tranquility but here too they find no repose and equanimity. They are nowhere men in quest of a somewhere place. They grope about in a blind alley. Confronted by the self and problems of existence, they fall into the labyrinthine flux of life and become searingly aware of the inevitability of death, its tragic finality and existential certainty. Hence, their search for identity, for authentic selfhood, in the teeth of debilitating and disintegrating socio-political forces, is doomed to end in fiasco. They compromise but not with life and creativity, but with death and destructivity.

The novels of Arun Joshi successfully reveal the subtleties and complexities of modern life. They have excelled in exemplifying the existential dilemma of the self in the society. As Edmund Fuller observes : "In our age man suffers not only from persecution, famine and ruin but from an inner problem ... a conviction of isolation, randomness (and) meaninglessness in his way of existence" (*Man in Modern Fiction* : 03). In Joshi, this meaninglessness leads to the search for identity, "a perpetual quest for reality" (Trilling, 1953 : 2055. The Joshi, protagonists explore that mysterious underworld which is the human soul. His novels delineate the spiritual agony of his lonely questers. To Joshi, life's meaning lies not "in the glossy surfaces of pretentions but in the dark mossy labyrinths of the soul" (Pathak, "Quest for Meaning in Arun Joshi's Novels", The Novels of Arun Joshi : 74).

Sindi Oberoi, observes O.P. Bhatnagar, has "a strange feeling of aloneness and aloofness..." ("A Critique of East and West", *The Journal of Indian Writing in English*, July 1973, 13-14). But Meenakshi Mukherjee views Sindi as "a perennial outsider" (Qtd. in *Twice Born Fiction,* p. 22). In the long run, Sindi realises that his foreignness lay within him and was an integral part of him. His obsession with the notion of detachment makes him shirk his responsibility. Like Camus's Meursault, he is always bored with the world and like Neil of Philip Roth's *Good Bye, Columbus*, he does not want to shoulder even ordinary responsibilities. In a revolt against the societal preconceived values and traditions, he adopts an attitude of non-attachment. In *The Strange Case of Billy Biswas* the protagonist Billy rebels against the sham bourgeois society and its artificial way of living.

He is attracted towards the ancient and primitive forces of pristine sublimity. In a revolt against the modern life and its hollow meaninglessness he takes refuge in the arms of Bilasia amidst the tribal people. Ratan in *The Apprentice* gets swallowed in the dirty, murky waters of corruption despite his better self. His patriotic feelings get crumpled under the burden of joblessness, poverty and hunger. But when realisation dawns on him, he takes to shoe-shinning to redeem his past misdeeds. Although Ratan is steeped in corruption, he lashes out against corruption in his writings in journals and newspapers. These confessional expressions are the revolts of his overburdened soul. *The Last Labyrinth* explores the turbulent inner world of a wealthy young Indian, Som Bhasker. The diverse influences of his mother's spirituality and father's rational scientific theories confuse his mind. His soul always cries out for something of which he is himself unaware. He clamours after wealth and lust without finding any peace of mind. The search for spiritual bliss and a true identity becomes the goal of his life. All the angst ridden protagonists of Joshi are relentlessly in search of an identity unblemished by the filth of the modern corruption and its degenerating forces. They flounder through the labyrinthine lanes of their inner psyche to reach some sort of illumination.

Madhusudan Prasad observes : "They (Joshi's Novels) are singularised by certain existentialist problems and the resultant anger, agony, psychic quest and the like" (*Indian English Novelists : 51*).

Commenting on *The Last Labyrinth*, Walter says "Arun Joshi plungs deeper into the depths of the eternal queries that have perplexed man's consciousness from time immemorial" ("Arun Joshi's Vision of Life, Love, God and Death in *The Last Labyrinth*", *Studies in Indian Fiction in English* : 46) and we agree with the critics since in Joshi the search for identity is spiritual stemming from a rebellion against the degenerating forces of the society. Billy questions ".... Why this constant blurrings of reality? Who am I? Who are my parents? My wife? My child? (*The Strange Case of Billy Biswas* : 93). This question reveals Billy's spiritual quest for a true identity which has been haunting human minds since eternity. Although critics say that Joshi's *The City and the River* focuses on the aspect of authenticity and is different from his earlier novels, we do not agree with them. Like Joshi's earlier works, *The City and the River* is also based on the individual search for his true self

Thus, we can conclude that in Joshi's novels the search for identity assumes personal dimension and is related to the growth of the individual's inner self.

WORKS CITED

Bannerji, Purabi. "Interview with Joshi", The Sunday Statesman Feb. 27, 1983, qtd. by R.K. Dhawan, *The Functional World of Arun Joshi* (New Delhi : Classical Publishing Co., 1986).

Bhatnagar, O.P. "Arun Joshi's The Foreigner : A Critique of East & West" *JIWE*, 1/2 (July 1973), pp. 13-14 Quoted by S.P. Swain in "Sindi Oberoi: Arun Joshi's Alienated Hero in The Foreigner" in R.E. Dhawan (ed.) Indian Literature Today, Vol. (N. Delhi : Prestige, 94).

Dua., M.P. "Reply of Joshi", Sept. 3, 1971, qtd. by R.K. Dhawan, *op. cit.*

Fuller, Edmund. *Man in Modern Fiction* (New York : Random House, 1958).

Iyengar, K.R.S. *Indian Writing in English* (New Delhi : Sterling, 1985).

Joshi, Arun. *The Foreigner*, New Delhi : Hind, 1968.

— *The Strange Case of Billy Biswas*, New Delhi : Hind, 1971.

— *The Apprentice*, New Delhi : Orient Paperbacks, 1974.

— *The Last Labyrinth,* New Delhi : Vision, 1981.

— *The City and the River*, New Delhi : Orient Paperbacks, 1994.

Mukherjee, Meenakshi. *The Twice Born Fiction* (New Delhi : Heinemann, 1971).

Pathak, R.S. "Quest for Meaning in Arun Joshi's Novels" in Dhawan (ed). *The Novels of Arun Joshi* (New Delhi : Prestige, 1992).

Prasad, Madhusudan. "Arun Joshi", *Indian English Novelists* (New Delhi : Sterling, 1982).

Trilling, Lionel. *The Liberal Imagination* (New York : Doubleday, 1953).

Walter, Inna. "Arun Joshi's Vision of Life, Love, God and Death in The Last Labyrinth" in Balarama Gupta (ed.) *Studies in Indian Fiction in English*, (Gulbarga : JIWE's Publns., 1987).

13

Arun Joshi's Fictional Forte

MALLIKARJUN PATIL

The age after Mulk Raj Anand, R.K. Narayan and Raja Rao, the great trio of the Indian novel in English, saw the entry of a host of young and enthusiastic Indo-Anglian novelists. The younger generation of novelists who came on to the scene after the mid-twentieth century, are Manohar Malgonkar, Arun Josh, G.V. Desani, Anita Desai, Ruth Prawer Jhabvala, Salman Rushdie, Khushwant Singh and so on. These modern novelists — strong and prolific — are influenced by the second World War, Independence of India, women's emancipation, and a sense of alienation, rootlessness and a host of existential issues. These second generation writers of Indo-Anglian fiction, largely influenced by the Western style of life and ideas, began to write novels in the line of nineteenth century British writers like Charles Dickens and Thomas Hardy. Besides, the problem of how to lead a peaceful and productive life led them to think about man, his way of life, the means he has to employ and other problems. In this respect the works of present day Indo-Anglian novelists resemble the works of Camus, Sartre and Kafka. Among the writers who qualify as existentialist writers, Arun Joshi is the first and the finest one. His works evidence a strong influence of Camus and Sartre. His fictional world is characterized by frustration, disintegration and a sense of alienation. Like Joseph Conrad and V.S. Naipaul, Arun Joshi seems to be preoccupied with the themes of man's existence, bad faith and aimlessness life. In the words of Hari Mohan Prasad, "His novel is both a chronicle of chaos and a mode of quest."[1]

Arun Joshi's first novel *The Foreigner* was published in 1968. In fact, it was written two years earlier when he was a student in an American University. The novel, like many of Ruth Prawer Jhabvala's novels is about the East-West Encounter. The other aspects it covers are quest for a 'meaningful stance of life,' 'rootlessness' and so on. Sindi Oberoi, the protagonist of the novel is a product of the East and West. He is born of an English woman and a Kenyan-Indian father. So he is a child of mixed parentage. Besides, he is an orphan as his illustrious parents die in a plane crash. He is brought up by an uncle in Kenya. Rootless as he is, he travels worldwide — first to London for education, then to Boston for job and lastly to New Delhi for self-realization. He gets his education in London where he falls in love with Anna, a minor Soho artist. Like a stranger and rootless man, a la Camus's *Outsider*, he goes as a wanderer. Denied of love, familial nourishment and cultural roots, he seeks fulfilment wherever it is possible. He becomes a lone sojourner. He calls himself "an uprooted young man living in the latter half of the twentieth century who had detached from everything except himself."

In London, although he is in love with Anna, he sleeps with Kathya. But Sindi's split personality and eccentric behaviour convinces them to part ways with him. As a result, Anna leaves him in quest of something else and Kathya leaves him for the sacredness of marriage. Later he goes to Boston where he completes his education and does some business. It is in Boston that he falls in love with June, a benign and beautiful lady. Their love matures and at a point of time when she wants to marry him, he dislikes it. As a consequence, June marries Babu, an Indian. But when Babu comes to know the fact that June had been in love with Sindi too, he commits suicide. June too dies later. Hari Mohan Prasad calls this phase of cross-sectional life a symbol of 'cultural lag.' The character of Babu is simple, but the persona of June is complex; and Sindi is responsible for the death of both. At the end of the novel we see Sindi living in Delhi in the company of Sheila and Khemka. His life is delineated as a web of complicated relationships. His rootlessness and inconstancy, his ignorance and eccentricity, all lead him to bad faith or what Sartre calls 'Mauvaise force.'

Sindi is an eccentric and self-alienated person. His sense of detachment, lack of any basic and life-sustainable values and good nature or demeanour always land him in trouble. His predicament is spelt in clear terms in his dialogue with Khemka:

> But you at least knew what made an ass of a man; we don't even know that. You had a clear-cut system of morality, a caste system that laid down all. You had to do. You had a God: you had roots in the soil you lived upon. Look at me, I have no roots. I have no systems of morality. What does it mean to me if you call me an immoral man. I have no reason to be one thing rather than another. You ask me why I am not ambitious; well, I have no reason to become, to think of it. I don't even have a reason to live (135-36).

However, Sindi is an emotional figure. But his eccentricity, lust and rootlessness are harrowing. About Sindi, Hari Mohan Prasad remarks: "His life in Kenya, London or Boston and the varied experiences he undergoes illustrate his predicament of anomie and its further deepening into ontological insecurity."[2] The novel ends with Sindi's understanding of life's realities. He is like G.V. Desani's Hatter, a frustrated and self-alienated figure who, despite his efforts, does not get fulfilment in life.

Arun Joshi's second novel *The Strange Case of Mr. Billy Biswas* was published in 1971, three years after *The Foreigner*. But the theme of the novel is again the same Bimal Biswas; popularly known as Billy Biswas, a Banjara Indian by caste, is the hero of the novel. He has studied anthropology at Columbia and lives in America. He is well settled there. The novel shows the continuation of the theme, *viz.*, search for self-realization which abruptly came to an end in *The Foreigner*. However, the character of Billy Biswas is much different from Sindi Oberoi.

Billy Biswas is a pagan, a premitive man. He is a tribal personality by taste and temperament and an urbanised individual only in his outward appearance. He is educated in America but he dislikes the corrupt modern civilization. According to him the material reality is not good for a peaceful and productive co-existence. He thinks that sex too is poisonous if it is not maintained judiciously. His idea of sexuality is that excessive sexual intercourse or lust is dangerous not only for physical health but also for mental harmony. Billy Biswas does not like the artificial mode of life prevalent in Amcrica. As a matter of fact, he is a stranger to the civilized world. In Billy's view modern civilization is a monster, and it certainly degrades human co-existence and weakens man's moral fibre. He boldly asserts:

> I sometimes wonder whether civilization is anything more than the making and spending of money. What else the civilized men do? And if there are those who are not busy earning and spending — the so-called thinkers and philosophers and men like that — they are merely hired to find solution, throw light, as they say, on complications caused by this making and spending of money (97).

Billy Biswas comes across Meena Mukherjee who falls in love with him. Though he is eccentric in behaviour, she marries him. But their life does not run smoothly. The prime reason for this appears to be her seeking material prosperity. Similarly, he does not like Rima Kaul, sensuous and fascinating girl of Indian origin. He thinks neither Meena nor Rima Kaul is a lady meant for him as both differ from him a great deal. If Meena is in quest of material wealth, Rima Kaul is searching for sexual ecstasy. While Billy wants primitive happiness which his primeval ancestors aspired. Then he finds Bilasia, a woman of his own taste and temperament. He finds happeness in her company. Each finds real partner now. They enjoy each other's companionship to the full. His happiness is indescribable. "When Bilasia," Hari Mohan Prasad affirms, "makes herself available to him, he does not feel that it is a union of flesh as with Rima. It is merging of a split-self to realize the whole."[3]

Billy Biswas is a Gandhian as far as his understanding of the present civilization goes; a Wordsworthian as he finds happiness in trible life of simplicity and grace. He is thoroughly simplistic in his search of divine values. He thinks Man's greed for materialistic values will take him nowhere. Talking of the civilization and corrupt society around him, he tells Romi, his friend:

> I don't think I have ever met a more pompous, a more mixed-up lot of people. Artistically, they were

> dry as dust. Intellectually, they could do no better than mechanically mouth ideas that the West abandoned a generation ago. Their idea of romance was to go and see an American movie or go to one of those wretched restaurants and dance with their wives to a thirty year old tune. Nobody remembers the old songs or the meaning of the festivals. All the sensuality was gone. So was the poetry. All that was left was loudmouthed women and men in three piece suits dreaming their little adulteries (197).

The novel is a brilliant satire on modern civilization. Like Thomas Moore's *Utopia,* it successfully portrays the old idealistic mode of life. That is why the hero is called "The Primitive Pilgrim."[4] R.K. Dhawan observes that the novel is about a mystical urge. Commenting on his first two novels Arun Joshi states, "Both these novels are primarily concerned with religious issues — the problems of an essentially Hindu mind."[5]

Arun Joshi's next novel *The Apprentice* is a very powerful work of art that holds mirror to the present-day life. It is a work of a mature novelist written in the confessional mode. In this regard, *The Apprentice* resembles R.K. Narayan's *The Guide.* But the essential difference between the two novels is that if Ratan, the protagonist of *The Apprentice* swerves from the right path to the wrong, Raju, the rouge hero of *The Guide* follows the opposite course. However, both the heroes repent and regret their 'fallenness.'

The story of the novel is the 1940s struggle for Independence. Ratan's father Rathod sacrifices everything and participates in the freedom struggle and one day when he is in procession against the British, he becomes a martyr due to a police's bullet. In course of time the nation becomes liberated from the shackles of the foreign rule. But what goes wrong is that the values of the pre-Independence India undergo a total change and the complete ideal mode of life is just reversed. Good people begin to follow the favourable means for favourable ends. They forget the fact that means are equally important as the ends. They work to become rich and respectable regardless of the means they employ for the realisation of their desires.

Then Ratan becomes a responsible man in the family as his mother, a widow, cannot shoulder the many responsibilities herself. He searches for a job. His friends, those who admired his father's martyrdom and the politicians of the independent India pretend to help him. But to his surprise none really helps. Ratan, an honest and virtuous man, realizes the gravity of the situation he finds himself in owing to his goodness, love of truth and the like. Now he changes his stance. He begins to tell lies, pretends in accordance to the need, and follows favourable means for a happy life. Thus, easily he gets a job. His officer sees to it that his cousin's daughter marries him. His material status dramatically improves. But mentally he is in doldrums as his consciousness is always split like that of Sindi or Billy. He repents his depersonalization caused by the materialism of modern science and commerce:

> I had become, at the age of twenty one, hypocrite and a liar, in short, a sham.... From morning till night I told more lies than truths. I had become a master faker (28).

According to H.M. Prasad and K.R.S. Iyengar the failure of faith in nobility, education, justice, friendship and hard work shocked him earlier, but at present he becomes one of those who sees that the old values are useful no more. But now he regrets and repents his past deeds. He becomes restless. He makes compromises, but every compromise gnaws at his conscience. For instance when he goes to a temple, he is bribed by a pujari to give a job to the pujari's son.

The novel is confessional tone. It exposes the evils of the world. Iyengar rightly observes: "As a fictional study of the anatomy and dynamics of the almost omnipresent corruption in the country, *The Apprentice* is a powerful indictment. The human story and the stark message both come through." Indeed, the novel is a powerful social document and a "threnody of a tormented soul" of modern world.

Arun Joshi's recent novel *The Last Labyrinth* is a study of modern man's mental tumult. It treats man's split state of mind and its causes and consequences. It portrays a modern Hamlet whose problem is to become materialistic or spiritualistic.

Som Bhaskar is a young and educated business tycoon. In fact, the novel is autobiographical. It depicts Som Bhaskar's quest for both physical and mental fulfilments in life. However, his desire for materialistic comforts as well as mental harmony takes him nowhere. *The Last Labyrinth* explores the crannies of Som, his Jungian and Sartrean struggle for an authentic mode of life. His mind is a labyrinth and so are his life, ambition, reality and existence.

The reasons for Som Bhaskar's erratic way of life are many and varied. His family background is the *primum mobile* for his present situation in life. His grandfather was a happy, fun loving man. He was a womanizer and a lazy man. He led a happy life. He never worried about God or heaven. Som's father was different from his grandfather. He was an educated man, a brilliant scholar and a scientist. But Som Bhaskar, is a harmonious blend of his father and grandfather. Like the latter he is a womaniser, and like the former he is a rationalist. However, he appears to be a compound of two elements, he behaves like an inert gas — not at all co-existing with Geeta, his wife, Leela Sabnis, his lover, and Anuradha, whom he pursues. He does not find fulfilment in Geeta's serene company. Nor does is he happy in Leela Sabnis's company, who is a sensual and rational woman and who understands him. When he aspires for otherwordliness, different from the materialism of Leela, she tells him, "You haven't got the stamina, for that, I know. You haven't got the faith. You have always been a sceptic. You always will be."[6]

Like Billy Biswas he goes in search of the otherworldliness. But in Som Bhaskar's case it is not 'primitivism' but 'spiritualism.' So he befriends Gargi, Aftab and Anuradha. These three people are truly like Indian saints, like Sabrai of Khushwant Singh's novel *I Shall Not Hear the Nightingale.*

They are warm hearted and well-cultured. Neither Gargi nor Aftab, nor Anuradha have committed any unpardonable mistakes in life. All are unmarried and pure. But Anuradha, a woman who, like June of *The Foreigner,* wants to help all regardless of her own happiness; shares Bhaskar's bed to please him. However, it does not lower her image in the view of her friends or the readers. Nevertheless, Bhaskar, the merry-go-lucky free lancer insists upon her being with him all the time. In allowing Som enjoy her,

Anuradha's intention is to inspire joy in him. Throughout the novel a keen observer can find that Som's quest is for fulfilment. H.M. Prasad calls this 'the pilgrims' progress.' But the degree of progress he makes is negligible. According to Prasad, "He develops an intense feeling of inadequacy, a feeling of rootlessness, a feeling of a rudderless boat being tossed on turbulent waves."[7]

Besides the novels, Arun Joshi has written *The Survivor,* a collection of short stories. His stories like "The Survivor," "The Gherao" and "Harmik" evidence his excellent craftmanship, vivid mode of narration and mature style. These works of Arun Joshi, according to scholars like R.K. Dhawan, O.P. Bhatnagar, V. Gopal Reddy and others, are signs of his mature genius, skilled narrative style and profound vision of life.

NOTES

1. Hari Mohan Prasad, *Arun Joshi* (New Delhi: Arnold-Heinemann, 1985), 9.
2. Prasad, 30.
3. Prasad, 58.
4. Prasad, 46.
5. Quoted in R.K. Dhawan, *The Fictional World of Arun Joshi*, ed. by R.K. Dhawan (Delhi: Classic Publishing Company, 1986) 20.
6. Arun Joshi, *The Last Labyrinth* (New Delhi: Orient Paperbacks, 1981), 114.
7. Prasad, 88-89.

Bibliography

A. PRIMARY SOURCES

Novels

The Foreigner. Bombay : Asia Publishing House, 1968. Delhi : Hind Pocket Books, 1972.

The Strange Case of Billy Biswas. Bombay : Asia Publishing House, 1971. Delhi : Hind Pocket Books, 1973.

The Apprentice. New York : Asia Publishing House, 1974. Delhi : Hind Pocket Books, 1975. Bombay : Asia Publishing House, 1975.

The Last Labyrinth. New Delhi : Vision Books, 1981.

The City and the River. New Delhi : Vision Books, 1990.

Short Stories

The Survivor : A Selection of Stories. Delhi : Sterling Publishers, 1975.

Interviews

Banerjee, Purabi. "A Winner's Secret" An Interview. *Sunday Statesman* (Calcutta) 27 Feb, 1983 : IV.

Excerpts from a Talk by Arun Joshi at Dhvanyaloka, Mysore. Sep. 1981. *ACLALS Newsletter* No. 10 Jan. 1982.

Mathai, Sujata. "I'm a stranger to my books." An Interview. *Times of India* 7 July 1983 : 8.

Piciucco, Pier Paolo. An Interview with Arun Joshi. *Journal of Indian Writing in English* 25.1-2 (1997). 87-95.

B. SECONDARY SOURCES : CRITICAL WORKS

Bibliographies

Srivastava, Ramesh K., comp. "Arun Joshi : Selected Bibliographies. *Six Indian Novelists in English.* Amritsar: Guru Nanak Dev Unversity, 1987 : 351-353.

Special Issues

Scholar Critic 1984. Rpt. as *Arun Joshi : A Study of His Fiction.* Ed. N. Radhakrishnan. Gandhigram : Scholar Critic Publications, 1984.

Books

Dhawan, R.K., ed. *The Fictional World of Arun Joshi.* New Delhi : Classical Publishing Company, 1986.

Dhawan, R.K., ed. *The Novels of Arun Joshi.* New Delhi: Prestige Books, 1992.

Ghosh, Tapan Kumar. *Arun Joshi's Fiction : The Labyrinth of Life.* New Delhi : Prestige Books, 1996.

Prasad, Hari Mohan. *Arun Joshi.* New Delhi : Arnold Heinemann, 1985.

Radhakrishnan, N. *Arun Joshi : A Study of His Fiction.* Gandhigram : A Scholar Critic Publication, 1984.

Rajendra Prasad, Ch. A. *The Function of Enigma in Arun Joshi : A Critial Study.* Narasapur (Andhra Pradesh, India) : Privately Published, 1996.

Research Articles

Abraham, Joy. "Vision and Technique in *The Apprentice.*" Dhawan, *The Fictional World of Arun Joshi* 210-222.

——. "*The Foreigner* : A Study in Techniques." Dhawan, *The Novels of Arun Joshi.* 143-161.

——. "Narrative Strategy in *The Strange Case of Billy Biswas.*" Dhawan, *The Novels of Arun Joshi.* 191-200.

Abraham, P.A. "Patrick White's Voss and Arun Joshi's *The Strange Case of Billy Biswas* : A Comparative Note on a Journey into the Interior." *Literary Criterion* 27.4 (1992) : 22-30.

Alam, Qaiser Joha. "The Image in Arun Joshi's Fiction" *Language and Literature* 33-44.

Asnani, Shyam M. "A Study of Arun Joshi's Fiction." *Literary Half-Yearly* 19.2 (1978) : 98-114. Rpt. in Asnani, *New Dimensions* 63-77.

Awasthi, Kamal N and Lalit M. Sharma. "The World of 'Outsiders' in *The Foreigner* and *Voices in the City.*" Awasthi 104-114.

Bande, Usha. "Anita Desai, Arun Joshi and Anasakti Yoga." *Language Forum* 14.1 (1988) : 54-64. Rpt. in Dhawan, *The Fiction of Anita Desai,* 54-65.

——. "Archetypal Patterns in *The City and the River.*" Dhawan, *The Novels of Arun Joshi* 257-264.

——. "Victor-Victim Syndrome in Arun Joshi's *The City and the River.*" Bande, *Victim Consciousness* 106-113.

——. "Symbolism in Arun Joshi's *The Last Labrynth.*" Srivatsava, R.K., *Symbolism* 150-162.

Bano, Hamida. "The Quest for True Self in Arun Joshi's *The Foreigner.*" *English Studies in India* 3 (1988) : 112-122.

Beniwal, Anup. "A Stylistic Insight into *The Last Labyrinth.*" Dhawan, *The Novels of Arun Joshi.* 230-240.

——. "*The City and the River* : A Critical Review." Dhawan, *The Novels of Arun Joshi.* 274-275.

Bhatnagar, O.P. "Arun Joshi's *The Foreigner.*" *Journal of Indian Writing in English* 1.2 (1973) : 9-14.

——. "The Art and Vision of Arun Joshi." *Scholar Critic* 4.6 (1984) : 30-43. Rpt. in Dhawan, *The Fictional World of Arun Joshi* 49-68.

Chakravarthy, D.K. "Rathan Rathor's Search for the Last Outpost : An Approach to Arun Joshi's *The Apprentice.*" Chakravorthy 35-44.

——. "Waiting for Moonrise : An Approach to Arun Joshi's novel, *The Strange Case of Billy Biswas.*" Chakravorthy, 45-48.

Chandar, K.M. "The Quest for Faith in Arun Joshi's *The Last Labyrinth.*" *Sinha and Sinha* 56-62.

Chandra, Subhash. "Towards authenticity : A Study of *The City and the River.*" Dhawan, *The Novels of Arun Joshi* 265-273.

Chandra, Suresh. "The High Culture Fiction of Arun Joshi and Uma Vasudev." Chandra 99-109.

Chingre, C.D. "Contrast as Technique in Arun Joshi's *The Strange Case of Billy Biswas.*" *Indian Journal of English Studies* 30 (1991-92) : 79-84.

——. "Woman characters in the Novels of Arun Joshi." *Commonwealth Review* 6.1 (1994-95) : 155-158. Rpt. in Dass, *Feminism and Literature* 155.

Damodar, G. "The Outsiderist Tradition in Joshi and Desai " *Kakatiya Journal of English Studies* 13 (1993) : 59-66.

Das, R.J. "Moral Dilemma in Arun Joshi's *The Apprentice.*" *Journal of Literature and Aesthetics* 1.2 (1981) : 39-45.

Devi, P. Janiki. "Search for Identity in the Novels of Arun Joshi." *Journal of English Studies* (Warangal) 10.1 (1978) : 620-627.

Dhawan, R.K. "The Fictional World of Arun Joshi." Dhawan, *The Fictional World of Arun Joshi* 17-48.

——. "Destiny of a Nation : Arun Joshi's *The Apprentice.*" Pandey and Raj Rao 51-60.

Dutta, Padma. "Problems of Individuation : A Critique on Arun Joshi's Use of Symbols and Archetypes in *The Last Labyrinth.*" *Journal of Indian Writing in English* 18.1 (1990) : 31-40.

Dwivedi, A.N. "The Novels of Arun Joshi : A Critical Study." Dwivedi, *Studies in Contemporary Indian Fiction in English* 309-318.

Gautam, Hansa. "Tension and Tonicity in Arun Joshi's Novels." *Contour* 1.2-3 (1992) : 10-15.

Gopala Krishna, M.G. "The Short Stories of Arun Joshi." *Scholar Critic* 4.6 (1984): 68-73. Rpt. in Radhakrishnan, *Arun Joshi* 68-73.

Guruprasad, Thakur. "The Lost Lonely Questers of Arun Joshi's Fiction." Dhawan, *The Fictional World of Arun Joshi.* 155-166.

Hegde, M.G. "Distance and Discovery as Techniques : A Study of the Narrative Strategy of *The Strange Case of Billy Biswas.*" *Osmania Journal of English Studies* 25 (1989) : 92-100.

——. "Arun Joshi's Lala Shri Ram : A Study." *Journal of Indian Writing in English* 17.2 (1989) : 18-22.

——. "The Short Stories of Arun Joshi : A Study." Dhawan, *The Novels of Arun Joshi* 201-209.

Jain, Jasbir. "Foreigners and Strangers : Arun Joshi's Heroes." *Journal of Indian Writing in English* 5.1 (1977) : 52-56.

Jamkhandi, Sudhakar R. "Arun Joshi : An Emerging Voice in Indian English Literature." *Literary Endeavour* 4.1-4 (1985) : 36-44.

Jha, Mohan. "*The Foreigner* : A Study in Innocence and Experience." Dhawan, *The Fictional World of Arun Joshi* 168-175.

Jeevan, Parvathy. "Image of Woman in the Novels of Arun Joshi." *Commonwealth Quarterly* 16.41 (1980) : 24-34. Rpt. in *Littcrit* 16.1-2 (1992) : 85-92.

——. "Arun Joshi : Master of Science and Letters." *Malayalam Literary Survey* 13.3 (1991) : 25-29.

Joshi, Surender. "Point of view and Theme in Arun Joshi's *The Strange Case of Billy Biswas.*" Saxena, *Glimpses* Vol. 3. 70-79.

Kalinnikova, Elena J. "In Search of Anti-Hero : Anita Desai and Arun Joshi." Kalinnikova *Indian English Literature : A Perspective.* 174-178.

Kher, Inder Nath. "The Archetypes of Love and Death in Arun Joshi's *The Last Labyrinth.*" *Journal of Indian Writing in English* 20.1-2 (1992) : 53-66.

Kumar, Sunaina. "A Tribute : Arun Joshi and His Extraordinary Obsessions." *Indian Book Chronicle* June 1993 : 20.

Mathur, O.P. "From Existentialism to Karma Yogi : A Study of Arun Joshi's *The Foreigner.*" Srivastava, A.K. *Alien Voice* 107-115. ref. : 524.

——. "Survival and Affirmation in Arun Joshi's Novels." *Worlds Literature Today* 63.3 (1989) : 421-425.

——. "Arun Joshi's *The City and The River* : A Leap to eternity." Mathur, *Indian Political Novel* 91-101.

——. "The contemporary and The Cosmic and in Arun Joshi's *The City and the River.*" Yaravintelimath *et al*, 147-153.

——. "Arun Joshi and The Gita." Pathak, *Indian English Fiction* 132-145.

Mathur, O.P. and G. Rai. "The Existential Note in Arun Joshi's *The Strange Case of Billy Biswas* and *The Apprentice.*" *Commonwealth Quarterly* 5.17 (1980) : 30-41.

——. "Arun Joshi and the Labyrinth of Life." Dhawan, *The Fictional World of Arun Joshi* 143-154.

Meitei, M. Mani. "*The Strange Case of Billy Biswas* : Awareness of Worlds Within Worlds." *Quest* (Ranchi) 4.2 (1990) : 9-20.

——. "Indian Ethos in Arun Joshi's *The Last Labyrinth.*" *Language Forum* 19.1-2 (1992) : 160-172.

Mohan, Devinder. "The Image of Fire in Arun Joshi's *The Strange Case of Billy Biswas.*" Dhawan, *The Fictional World of Arun Joshi* 194-209.

——. "The Dance of Life and Death : Arun Joshi's Fiction." *Asia Week* 16 Aug. 1987.

——. "The Language of the Splintered Mirror : The Fiction of Arun Joshi." *Ariel* 14.4 (1983) : 20-33.

——. "Arun Joshi : *The Foreigner.*" Pradhan, 174-191.

——. "Beyond the Litany of Wants : Contexts of Arun Joshi's Fiction Towards *The Last Labyrinth.*" Kirpal, *The New Indian Novel in English* 83-90.

Mohanty, Mahendra Kumar. "Filial Relationships in *The Foreigner*" Dhawan, *The Novels of Arun Joshi* 115-121.

Narasimhaiah, Sanjay. "Arun Joshi's *The Last Labyrinth.*" *Literary Criterion* 15.2 (1981) : 81-89.

Padma, T. "Problems of Individuation : A Critique on Arun Joshi's Use of Symbols and Archetypes in *The Last Labyrinth.*" *Journal of Indian Writing in English* 18.1 (1990) : 31-40. Rpt. in Prabhakar 285-294.

——. Crypto-myth and Meta-novel : Arun Joshi's *The City and the River.*" Nair *et al* 107-115.

Pandey, Lal Udai Bhan. "Anita Desai and Arun Joshi : A Comparative Study." Dhawan, *Recent Commonwealth Literature* Vol. I. 224-226.

Pathak, R.S. "Arun Joshi's Novels : An Indeterminate Search for Meaning in Life." *Scholar Critic* 4.6 (1984): 44-63. Rpt. in

Radhakrishnan, *Arun Joshi* : 44-63. Rpt. as "Human Predicament and Meaninglessness in Arun Joshi's Novels (An enlarged and restructured version)." Dhawan, *The Fictional World of Arun Joshi* 104-142.

——. "Quest for Meaning in Arun Joshi's Novels." Dhawan, *The Novels of Arun Joshi* 42-82.

Pathania, Usha. "Having and Being : A Study of *The Foreigner.*" Dhawan, *The Novels of Arun Joshi* : 133-142.

——. "The Quest for Being : An Analysis of *The Foreigner.*" Kaul & Jaidev 159-166.

Patnaik, B.N. "What is Strange in *The Strange Case of Billy Biswas.*" *Gray Book* 3 (1973) : 17-24.

Piciucco, Pier Parlo. "Fictional Technique and Rhetorical Devices in Arun Joshi's *The Apprentice.*" *Literary Criterion* 34.2 (1999) : 30-43.

Prabhakaran, M.S. "The Apprentice : An Overview." *Scholar Critic* 4.6(1984) : 64-67. Rpt. in Radhakrishnan, *Arun Joshi* 64-67.

Prasad, Hari Mohan. "The Crisis of Consciousness : A Thematic Analysis of *The Last Labyrinth.*" *Scholar Critic* 4.6 (1984) : 20-29. Rpt in Dhawan, *The Fictional World of Arun Joshi* 231-240.

Prasad, Madhusudan. "Arun Joshi : The Novelist." *Indian Literature,* July-Aug. 1981 : 103-114. Rpt. in Prasad, Madhusudan, *Indian English Novelists* 50-61.

——. "Cornering Arun Joshi : A Critical Perspective on *The Last Labyrinth.*" *Scholar Critic* 4.6 (1984) : 9-19. Rpt. in Radhakrishnan, *Arun Joshi* 9-19.

Prasad, V.V.N. Rajendra. "Arun Joshi : Self as Labyrinth." Prasad, V.V.N 108-129.

——. "*The Apprentice* : Self as Labyrinth." Dhawan, *The Novels of Arun Joshi* 210-216.

Prempati, D. "*The Strange Case of Billy Biswas* : A Serious Response to a Big Challenge." Dhawan, *The Fictional World of Arun Joshi* 176-185. ref. : 4037. Rpt. in Dhawan, *The Novels of Arun Joshi* 174-180.

Radha, K. "From Detachment to Involvement : The Career of the Chief protagonist to Arun Joshi's *The Foreigner.*" Paniker, *Contemporary Indian Fiction in English,* 81-90. Rpt. in Dhawan, *The Fictional World of Arun Joshi* 176-185. Rpt. as "From detachment to Involvement : The Case of Sindi Oberoi in Dhawan, *The Novels of Arun Joshi* 106-114

——. "Fugitive for Self and the City in Margaret Atwood's *Surfacing* and Some Indian Novels in English." Begum 21-32.

Radhakrishnan, N. "The Women Characters of Arun Joshi." *Scholar Critic* 4.6 (1984); 74-80. Rpt. in Radhakrishnan, *Arun Joshi* 74-80.

Raizada, Harish. "Double Vision of Fantasy and Reality in Arun Joshi's Novels." Dhawan, *The Fictional World of Arun Joshi* 69-103.

Rajendraprasad, Ch. A. "'After the Fall' : A critique on Arun Joshi's *The Apprentice.*" *Revaluations* 2.1(1996): 79-85.

Rengachari, S. "T.S. Eliot's Shadow on The Foreigners." *Scholar Critic* 4.6 (1984) : 1-8. Rpt. in Radhakrishnan, *Arun Joshi* 1-8.

Rangan. "The Theme of Alienation and Quest for Identity in Arun Joshi's *The Last Labyrinth.*" Nagarajan *et al.* 109-116.

Rani, Rekha. "The Language of Dreams in *The Last Labyrinth.*" Dhawan, *The Novels of Arun Joshi* 224-229.

Rao, M. Madhusudan. "The Hindu Existential Concern in Arun Joshi's Fiction." Rao, A. Ramakrishna and Sivaramkrishna 149-161.

Rao, Ramakrishna A. "Arun Joshi's Voids and Labyrinths." *Literary Endeavour* 2.4 (1981) : 11-17.

——. "The Image of Labyrinth in Borges, Durrell and Joshi." Saxena, *Glimpses* Vol. 3. 3-22.

Ratnakar, Pramesh. "Arun Joshi's Fiction : Cracks in the Mirror." *Occasional Papers in English and Linguistics* 2 (1985).

Reddy, V. Gopal. "The Apprentice : An Existential Study." *Kakatiya Journal of English Study.*" 5 (1983) : 9-16. Rpt. in Dhawan, *The Fictional World of Arun Joshi* 223-230.

——. "From Alienation to Community : A Note on the Novels of Arun Joshi." *Kakatiya Journal of English Studies* 7 (1985-86) : 82-91.

Ross, Robert. "The Clash of Opposites in Arun Joshi's *The Last Labyrinth.*" *Literary Criterion* 25.2 (1990) : 1-9.

Satapathy, S.C. "From Passivity to Awareness : A Study of the Narrator-Protagonist in Arun Joshi's *The Apprentice.*" *Journal of Literary Studies* 2.2 (1979) : 121-132.

Satyanarayana, E. "Towards Affirmation : A Reading of Arun Joshi's 'A Trip For Mr. Lee.' and 'Survivor'." Narendra Kumar, V.L.V.N. *New Perspectives* 108-112. Rpt. as "Arun Joshi's 'A Trip for Mr. Lele' and 'Survivor'." in *Triveni* 66.1(1997) : 30-33

Sharma, Brahma Dutt. "*The City and the River* as a Political Novel." Dhawan, *The Novels of Arun Joshi* 241-256.

Sharma, D.R. "Arun Joshi and His Reflective Insiders." *Panjab University Research Bulletin (Arts)* 7.2 (1976) : 125-134. Rpt. in *Literature East and West* 21.1-4 (1977) : 100-111. Also in *Indian P.E.N.* Sept.-Oct. 1977 : 1.

——. "The Fictional World of Arun Joshi." *Indian P.E.N.* 43, Sept.-Oct. 1977.1-5.

Sharma, Shyam Sundar. "The Two Worlds in *The Last Labyrinth.*" Dhawan, *The Fictional World of Arun Joshi* 240-248.

Sharma, Susheel Kumar. "Philosophical Reverberations in *The Foreigner.*" Dhawan, *The Novels of Arun Joshi* 122-132.

——. "*The Strange case of Billy Biswas* : A Psycho-graph of an Alienated Hero." Dhawan, *The Novels of Arun Joshi* 62-116.

Singh, Khushwant. "Arun Joshi." *Hindustan Times,* 24 Jan. 1981 : 9-8.

Singh, R.S. "Aloness Alone : Anita Desai and Arun Joshi." Singh R.S., *Indian Novel in English* 164-178.

Srinath, C.N. "The Fiction of Arun Joshi : The Novel of Interior Landscape." *Literary Criterion* 12.2-3 (1976) : 115-133. Rpt. in Srinath, 40-59.

——. "Crisis of Identity : Assertion and Withdrawal in Naipaul and Arun Joshi." *Literary Criterion* 14.1(1979): 33-41. Rpt. in Srinath, 66-67.

——. "Native Roots and Novel Foliage : An Understanding of the Achievement of Indian Fiction in English." *Literary Criterion* 21.1-2 (1986) : 60-85. Rpt. in Srinath 98-116.

——. "Arun Joshi's *The Apprentice* : The Novel of Our Times" Narendra Kumar V.L.V.N., *New Perspectives* 113-117.

Srivastava, Narasingh. "Quest for Identity in Arun Joshi's *The Last Labyrinth.*" *Language Forum* 18.1 (1992) : 81-86.

Srivastava K. Ramesh. "The Theme of Alienation in Arun Joshi's Novels." *Ken : A Journal of English Studies* 1(1982) : 13-23. Rpt. in Srivastava, *Six Indian Novelists in English* 311-325.

——. "Intricate Alleys in Arun Joshi's *The Last Labyrinth.*" *Indian Journal of English Studies* 28 (1989) : 5-12.

Tripathy, J.P. "From Raju to Billy : Changing Aspects of Self-hood." *Language Forum* 18.1-4 (1992) : 75-80.

Venkateswara Rao, J. "*The Foreigner :* An Existential Dilemma." *Triveni* 64.1-2 (1995) : 73-76.

Venugopal, C.V. and M.G. Hedge. "Soul's Progress from Innocence through Ignorance to Knowledge : A Study of *The Apprentice.*" *Kakatiya Journal of English Studies* (Warangal) 8 (1987-88) : 163-169.

Verma, K. D. "The Metaphysics and Meta Structure of Appearance and Reality in Arun Joshi's *The Last Labyrinth.*" *International Fiction Review* 21.1-2 (1994): 44-50.

——. "Alienation, Identity and Structure in Arun Joshi's *The Apprentice.*" *Ariel* 22.1 (1991) : 71-90.

Vijaya Kumar, T. "Allegory and the Negation of History : Arun Joshi's *The City and the River.*" Kirpal, *Postmodern Indian English Novel* 145-152.

Walter, Inna. "Arun Joshi's Vision of Life, Love, God and Death in *The Last Labyrinth.*" Gupta, *Studies* 46-60.

Wandrekar, Kalpana. "The Foreigner : Chaos of Cultural Confusion." Wandrekar 79-91.

Yadav, Kumkum. "The Importance of Being Billy —Victim(s) in Arun Joshi's *The Strange Case of Billy Biswas*." Bande, *Victim Consciousness* 94-105.

Reviews

Amur, G.S. "A New Parable." Rev. of *The City and the River*. *Indian Literature* 144 (1991) : 152-157.

Bhatnagar, O.P. Rev. of *The Foreigner*. *Journal of Indian Writing in English* 1.2 (1973) : 9-14.

Bandopadhyay, Manohar. Rev. of *The Strange Case of Billy Biswas*. *Patriot* 1 Aug. 1982.

D'Monte, Darryl. "A Hollow Rebel." Rev. of *The Strange Case of Billy Biswas*. *Times of India* 27 June 1971 : 10 : 5-7.

Daruwalla, Keki. Rev. of *The Last Labyrinth*. *Indian Literature* July-Aug. 1983 : 136-40.

Futehally, Laeeq. "Story-Telling." Rev. of *The Apprentice and The Survivor*. *Quest* 93, Mar.-Apr. 1975 : 93-94.

Hariharan, Gita. "A Political Parable." Rev. of *The City and the River*. *Indian Literature* 144 (1991).

Iyengar, K.R.S. "The Fiction of Arun Joshi." Rev. of *The Last Labyrinth*. *Humanities Review* 3.2 (1981) : 39-40.

Keating, H.R.F. Rev. of *The Last Labyrinth*. *Times Literary Supplement* 6 Aug. 1982 : 863.

Malathi Rao, C. Rev. of *The Foreigner*. *Literary Criterion* 8.4(1969) : 76-77.

Mathai, Anna Sujatha. "In Search of Meaning." Rev. of *The Last Labyrinth*. *Indian Book Chronicle* 16 June 1983 : 219-220.

Mazumdar, Shubra. Rev. of *The City and The River*. *Book Review* Jan.-Feb. 1991 : 28.

Mukherjee, Meenakshi. Rev. of *The Foreigner*. *Quest* 60, Sep.-Oct.(1969) : 101-103.

——. Rev. of *The Strange Case of Billy Biswas*. *Quest* 72, Sep.-Oct. 1971 : 121-124.

N.B. Rev. of *The Foreigner*. *Opinion Literary Quarterly* (India) 1 (1974) : 50-52, 54.

——. Rev. of *The Strange Case of Billy Biswas. Opinion Literary Quarterly* 1 (1974) : 50-52, 54.

Naikar, Basavaraj S. Rev. of *The Last Labyrinth. World Literature Today* 56.4 (1982) : 752-53.

R.S. Rev. of *Apprentice. Divine Life* (India) 12 Oct. 1975: 19.

Rao, K.S.N. Rev. of *The Strange Case of Billy Biswas. Books Abroad* 46.4 (1972) : 726.

——. Rev. of *The Apprentice. Books Abroad* 49.1 (1975): 185.

Rev. of *The Apprentice. Times of India* 25 June 1976 : 10.

Rev. of *The Foreigner. Times of India* 17 Sep. 1972 : 9.

Rev. of *The Foreigner. Thought* 24, 15 July 1972 : 18-19.

Rev. of *The Foreigner. Indian and Foreign Review* 15 July 1969 : 21-22.

Rev. of *The Last Labyrinth. National Herald* (Sunday) 22 Nov. 1981 : 4.

Saraiya, Indu. Rev. of *The Apprentice. Indian P.E.N.* 41.8 (1975) : 4-16.

Shettigara, Tina. "Entering the Maze." Rev. of *The Last Labyrinth. CRNLE Review Journal* 1 (1982) : 53-54.

Tonpe, Vaijayanti Savant. Rev. of *The City and the River. Seminar* 384 Aug. 1991 : 48.

Trivedi, Harish. "The Bitch Goddess." Rev. of *The Last Labyrinth. Book Review* Sep.-Oct. 1982 : 72-74.

Dissertations

Abraham, Joy. "Themes and Narrative Techniques in the Novels of Arun Joshi." Calicut U, 1991.

Bhuyar, R.S. "Arun Joshi : A Study of His Fiction." Amravati U, 1985.

Dubey, Amitabh. "Thematic Patterns and Structural Design in Arun Joshi's Novels." Dr. H.S. Gour U, 19?.

Hegde, Manjunath Gajanan. "Arun Joshi : A Study in Theme and Technique." Karnatak U, 1991.

Joshi, P.S. "Themes and Techniques of Arun Joshi's Novels." Diss. (M.Phil.). South Gujarat U, 1985.

Navaneethan, S. "Thematic Progression in the Novels of Arun Joshi." Bharathisadan U, 1985.

Pradhan, Shanta. "Modern Element in Indian English Fiction with Special Reference to the Novels of Raja Rao, Anita Desai and Arun Joshi." Gauhati U, 1990.

Prasad, V.V.N. Rajendra. "Self, Family and Society in the Novels of Rajan, Raja Rao, R.K. Narayan, Arun Joshi and Anita Desai." U of Krishnadevaraya, 1988. New Delhi : Prestige Books, 1990.

Rajendra Prasad, Chiliki Appala. "The Function of 'Enigma' in Arun Joshi's Novels." Andhra U, 1990.

Ranveer, P. Rukmani. "Encaged Sensibility in the Novels of Arun Joshi." Kakatiya U, 1990.

Satyanarayana, N. "New Morality in Indian-English Fiction with Special Reference to Anand, Narayan and Arun Joshi." Kakatiya U, 1987.

Contributors

M.K. Bhatnagar, Professor, Department of English, M.D. University, Rohtak.

A. Rajendra Prasad, Assistant Professor of English, University of Asmara, Asmara, Eritrea.

Pier Paolo Piciucco, Department of Foreign Languages, University of Turin, via S. Ottavio 19-10124 Turin, Italy.

Rashmi Gaur, Assistant Professor, Department of Humanities and Social Sciences, University of Roorkee, Roorkee.

Shivani Vatsa, Research Scholar, Department of Humanities, University of Roorkee, Roorkee.

Urmil, Teacher Fellow, Department of English, M.D. University, Rohtak.

M. Mani Meitei, Associate Professor of English, Manipur University, Canchipur, Imphal.

Rajeshwar Mittapalli, Associate Professor, Department of English, Kakatiya University, Vidyaranyapuri, Warangal.

B. Brahmananda Chary, Department of English, Kakatiya University, Vidyaranyapuri, Warangal and Vidyanagar College of Commerce, Hyderabad.

Shubha Tiwari, Senior Lecturer, Department of English, A.P.S. University, Rawa.

S.S. Rengachari, Head, Department of English, St. Mary's College, Tuticorin.

S.P. Swain and S. Samartray, Department of English, Rourkela Municipal College, Rourkela.

Mallikarjun Patil, Lecturer, Department of Studies in English, Gulbarga University, Gulbarga.